MW01076156

The Courtroom Ministry of Heaven

Dr. Randy Colver

PRESS

Copyright © 2003 by Dr. Randy Colver

The Courtroom Ministry of Heaven
by Dr. Randy Colver

Printed in the United States of America

Library of Congress Control Number: 2002115782
ISBN 1-591603-80-3

All rights reserved. No part of this publication may be reproduced or transmitted in any form or by any means without written permission of the publisher.

Scripture taken from the HOLY BIBLE, NEW INTER-NATIONAL VERSION®. NIV®. Copyright © 1973, 1978, 1984, by International Bible Society. Used by permission of Zondervan Publishing House. All rights reserved.

Xulon Press
www.XulonPress.com

Xulon Press books are available in bookstores everywhere, and on the Web at www.XulonPress.com.

Comments from Readers

"In his book, *The Courtroom Ministry of Heaven,* Dr. Randy Colver unveils for the reader a view of the heavenlies few have visualized. From the flurry of the celestial courtroom activity to the impact of these judicial pronouncements, the reader is transported to new levels of understanding and insight. Dr. Colver skillfully guides one to a view of heaven not soon forgotten."

Dr. Charles Travis, President
Logos Graduate School

"From the pen of a representative of the charismatic tradition, we now have a thoughtful and useful study, which documents how pervasively the Bible uses courtroom and legal notions and activities to elucidate the dealings of God with humanity. The Christian life—particularly prayer and the gift of prophecy—gains sharper focus and definition against the background which Colver ably provides."

Dr. Barry L. Blackburn
Professor of New Testament
Atlanta Christian College

"I found Dr. Colver's approach to be very unique and I feel this is a much-needed book on a subject rarely talked about. It was refreshing to focus on heaven and not earth. Dr. Colver has taken the reader on a journey right into the courtroom of heaven, thus inspiring all of us to look forward to the prize that is set before us, the fact that justice will be served based on the mercy and grace of our Lord."

Pastor Dick Iverson
Founder and President
Ministers Fellowship International

"We have used Dr. Colver's books both as texts and teaching materials. His attention to detail brings color and sound to the printed page, and his understanding of the Scriptures makes them speak. This book is no exception; the insight it gives into the courtroom procedures of heaven is excellent."

Dr. Eva B. Evans
Cornerstone Bible College

"Randy's intimate and holy walk with God is evidenced in this intriguing and enlightening look into the heavenlies that will keep you spellbound by the insights that God has revealed to him. His unique perspective concerning the operation of the gifts of the Holy Spirit for this present-day church and the difference between petitions and prayer are a must to read. I highly recommend this God-ordained book to any serious believer who has a hunger to know what is going on now, in the greatest of all courtrooms, with the greatest of all attorneys, Jesus Christ."

Frank Seamster
Evangelist and Revivalist

Acknowledgements

During my awakening years as a Charismatic, I read somewhere that there existed no comprehensive Charismatic Theology. This lack always seemed to be in the back of my mind as I poured over the Bible and read voraciously. Over the years, many excellent works on the gifts of the Spirit have appeared which have provided useful insights on this subject. I have also benefited from some superb teachers who gave me guidance on my journey: Dick Benjamin, Dick Strutz, and Jim Feeney, to name just a few, who kept me on track during my early Bible School years. Now it seems that gleaning from the many scholars of the Evangelical Theological Society fills the hunger of deeper cravings, though I have not forgotten my roots.

One has only to check the footnotes to realize that this work is built upon the valuable labors of many others—too numerous to begin to acknowl-edge. Perhaps it should be said only that I have pulled many "loose strands" together. Whether I have provided a framework for charismatic theology has yet to be seen. (After all, Christ said, "wisdom is proved right by *all* her children" [Lk. 7:35].)

I would be remiss not to mention the valuable services of my editor, Dale Glass-Hess, who painstakingly reviewed this monograph several times, without remuneration. Nor can I forget Professor Blackburn, who took time from his busy teaching schedule to offer several useful sugges-tions. George Vuduris deserves special thanks, for he underwrote this project, expecting nothing in return. And perhaps the person who deserves the most credit is my wife, Kim, who patiently put up with my constant drifting in thought and lack of attention dur-ing the years of writing this.

My deepest appreciation, of course, goes to my Lord and Savior. It is to His majesty that I readily and humbly cast any crowns, tarnished as they may be.

Contents

Introduction

Why Study the Courtroom Ministry of Heaven?

Not long after I received the Baptism of the Holy Spirit, the Lord gave me a spiritual dream.

I remember winds that whirled around me and lifted me up into dark, churning clouds. Christ appeared and spoke gracious, but authoritative words deep into my soul. When I awoke, my body trembled uncontrollably from the Lord's presence. Though what Christ spoke that day was personal correction, the dream caused me to know first-hand Christ's intimate relationship with each of us; and further, it left an indelible awareness of Christ's current ministry.

In times of quiet contemplation, these revelations stir within me as two of the greatest yearnings of the heart: *to know Christ intimately* and *to share in His ministry*. Since that dream, God has guided my Bible studies often in search of greater understanding of these two aspirations.

Recently, God brought Biblical concepts together along these two lines that before had seemed only remotely related. Themes regarding Christ's ministry from John, 1 Corinthians, and Hebrews, as well as from Job, the prophets, and the apocalyptic writings came together in new clarity. It was, in a sense, like the angel touching Elijah a second time and saying "Get up and eat, for the journey is too much for you." God had touched me again, this time nourishing my spirit by the truth of His Word. That revelation has sustained me far more than any other.

This revelation focuses on ministry in heaven. The glimpses Scripture gives us of heaven reveal a place of intense activity. Whether there be martyred saints petitioning the Father (Rev. 6:9-10), Divine Council members who deliberate on issues before the court (1 Kings 22:19-22; Ps. 89:7), angelic messengers (Rev. 8:2-6), prophetic visitors (Is. 6:1-4, 8-10; Rev. 4:1-2) or the multitude of heavenly hosts around the throne in worship (Rev. 5:11-13), almost every depiction of heaven portrays dynamic, vital ministry, full of the vibrant life of God.

The key to understanding these scenes of heaven lies in realizing that they center on the Divine Courtroom. Scripture narrates the activity of heaven largely as courtroom drama. By this I don't mean that we should conceive of heaven in the same way as we do a modern courtroom. The court of heaven functions in a much more regal manner. Perhaps the ancient court, where the king presided as judge, more closely resembles the heavenly model. Nevertheless, the Divine Court hears cases, renders verdicts, and carries out judgments, and we will examine this legal side in great detail throughout this monograph. In general, when I use the phrase "courtroom ministry of heaven," I refer to the legal aspects of God's activity in heaven—God's tribunal.

We cannot assume from this that heaven's legal court sits in session continually, but the record suggests significant courtroom ministry.

Further, understanding Christ's ministry in heaven comes in large part from understanding both the unique courtroom procedures of heaven and also the forensic terms depicting heaven or activity emanating from heaven. For the sake of a brief example, Daniel 7 records the kind of legal activity to which I refer:

> The *court was seated*, and *the books were opened*...As I watched, this horn was waging war against the saints and defeating them, until the Ancient of Days came and *pronounced judgment in favor* of the saints of the Most High, and the time came when they possessed the kingdom...*But the court will sit*, and his [the rebellious "horn's"] power will be taken away and completely destroyed forever.
> —Da. 7:21-22, 26 [emphasis added]

In this courtroom scene, a legal court session

begins with evidence presented to determine legitimate everlasting dominion. After due process, the Father gives the verdict in favor of the saints. The seating of the court suggests the finality of the decision.[1]

This heavenly courtroom is not a remote, undisclosed place, accessed only in "the sweet by-and-by." In fact, the Bible has a great deal to say about a Christian's unique connection to heaven. Scripture asserts that Christ blazed a trail to open the heavenlies for us (He. 10:19-22). Hence, we can approach the throne of grace to obtain mercy in time of need (He. 4:16). Paul said that God has "seated us with him in the heavenly realms in Christ Jesus" (Eph. 2:6) and that our citizenship originates from there (Phil. 3:19-20).

Since our "citizenship is of heaven," our existence must comply with heavenly jurisprudence. What the court decides in heaven must guide us. Let me give an example. The New American Standard Bible accurately translates Matthew 16:19 (cf. Mt. 18:18) as follows:[2]

> I will give you the keys of the kingdom of heaven; and whatever you shall bind on earth *shall have been bound in heaven*, and whatever you shall loose on earth *shall have been loosed in heaven.*

This verse shows that a Christian's empowerment comes from conformity to the will of heaven. In other words, for our petitions to have merit, we must first align them to the Judge's will. Thus, Christ declares that our legal authority as representatives of heaven derives from our adherence to the will of heaven. Lamentations affirms: "Who can speak and have it happen if the Lord has not decreed it?" (Lam. 3:37). Therefore, binding and loosing is not carte blanche authority for the Church, but rather the ability to act *according to* the authority of the Divine Court.

Commenting on the parallel passage of Matthew 18:18, the IVP Bible Background Commentary shows that Jews understood this derived legal authority:

> Many Jews felt that the Jewish high court acted on the authority of God's tribunal in heaven, in a sense ratifying its decrees (the verb tenses here also indicate that the heavenly court has decided first). Those who judged cases on the basis of God's law accurately represented his will.
>
> "Binding" and "loosing," terms normally used for tying up or imprisoning versus freeing or releasing, provide a natural metaphor for condemning or acquitting in a court.[3]

Though the Church does not conduct itself as a secular court, Christians act as representatives of heaven, giving testimony, or "witnessing" (a legal term), to heaven's decrees.

In similar fashion, the Lord's Prayer affirms our connection to heaven. When we pray, we should ask that the Father's will be done "on earth, as it is in heaven" (Mt. 6:10). Again, Isaiah records our prayer connection in legal terms, "'Present your case,' says the LORD. 'Set forth your arguments,' says Jacob's King" (Is. 41:21). From these cursory examples, we see that sharing in Christ's ministry through prayer is often rooted in the legal language of the court of heaven.

In the pages that follow, I hope to demonstrate in further detail the courtroom ministry of heaven and our vital connection to it. Our conception of heaven and its role in our lives should radically reorient our lives to Kingdom of Heaven living.

Are God's Legal Actions Important Today?

Large portions of the Bible relate both directly and indirectly to God's legal actions. God's precepts, commandments, judgments, and covenants make up the basis of our relationship with Him. "Indeed, the broad outline of the biblical narrative could be summarized as an extended judicial proceeding, going from the sin and punishment of Genesis to the final sifting of the Last Judgment."[4]

One may argue that since we base our relationship with God on love and worship we should not cast it in legal terms. However, the Bible juxtaposes love, worship, and God's legal actions without apology or contradiction. For instance, the Law is a practical expression of His love. Loving God and loving one another form the basis of Biblical laws.[5]

In addition, God's love finds its full expression in our lives only after legal obligations are met.

Scripture demonstrates this by the requirement of blood sacrifices as part of the Mosaic Covenant as well as by Christ's sacrifice as the basis for the New Covenant. The Law required substitutionary sacrifice for atonement of sins (Lev. 17:11). Unless this legal obligation was first met, no covenant love[6] with God could ensue.

As for worship, Israel often praised God after His judgments brought deliverance to the nation.[7] Even in the New Testament, worship follows judgment of sin[8] and proceeds from a heart redeemed and justified—two legal terms describing the new basis of our relationship. We must therefore learn to connect the dots from *judgment* of sin, to the *deliverance* that judgment brings, to the *worship* that results from deliverance. From Miriam's dance by the Dead Sea to the final Hallelujahs of Revelation, much of Biblical worship follows this progression. A God who justly judges sin connects each part until a clear picture of His purpose appears.

Others may argue that we base our relationship with God on grace and faith. Again, these are vitally important and necessary, but they are not antithetical to the foregoing. Did not God demonstrate His grace by establishing His covenants with humankind in the first place? In fact, God's covenants contain gratuitous promises of mercy and reconciliation.

This suggests that our relationship with God transcends a sterile business contract and that no artificial dichotomy exists between God's spiritual and legal actions.

Courtroom Ministry and Charismatic Theology

In addition to the above, I believe that studying the courtroom ministry of heaven has far-reaching implications for charismatic studies. While most "charismatic theologies" center on the ecstatic experiences themselves, or the renewal affect of such experiences, I have attempted in this study to provide a broader context within which the gifts of the Spirit play a role. Prophecy and other charismatic phenomena must be seen as an integral part of Christ's current ministry—not truncated, but understood as a vital means for God to achieve His overarching purposes.

Seen as part of the courtroom ministry of heaven, the gifts easily fit within the whole process of God's legal actions.

Layout of These Chapters

Finally, I would like to comment briefly on the presentation of this short monograph, which began originally as a technical paper on the courtroom ministry of heaven. The result of my scholarly approach leaves the first three chapters largely exegetical and theological. To some this may seem tedious reading—certainly more challenging than the average Charismatic study—but I've always believed that worthwhile reading should open new vistas not only of faith, but of thinking. Christ did, after all, admonish us to love the Lord "with all of our mind" as well. To others this will be a refreshing change of pace to the otherwise glut of Charismatic "cotton candy" in Christian bookstores.

The last chapter contains various ideas for applying this study, as well as several stories from recent experience. Too often scholarly studies fail to include this practical emphasis. Theology that misses the trenches should be left to collect dust and hold up other books on a bookshelf. My hope is that these principles and stories will provide a personal challenge to see our part in the courtroom ministry of heaven.

ENDNOTES

[1] See Da. 7:26; Mt. 19:28; He. 1:13; and Rev. 3:21.

[2] For a brief synopsis see D. A. Carson, **Exegetical Fallacies** (Grand Rapids: Baker, 1984) 79-80. See J. R. Mantey, *Evidence that the Perfect Tense in John 20:23 and Matthew 16:19 is Mistranslated*, **Journal of the Evangelical Theological Society** 16 (1973) 129-38.

[3] Craig Keener, *The IVP Bible Background Commentary: New Testament* (Downers Grove: InterVarsity Press, 1993) 94. See also Acts 22:5.

[4] Leland Ryken, James C. Wilhoit, Tremper Longman III, editors, *Dictionary of Biblical Imagery* (Downers Grove: InterVarsity Press, 1998).

[5] Deut. 6:5; 7:9; Mt. 22:37-40; Gal. 5:14.

[6] Hebrew "hesed."

[7] In Psalm 50 for instance, Asaph praised the virtues of God as Judge. God then addressed His people with judgment: "Hear, O my people, and I will speak, O Israel, and I will *testify against you*: I am God, your God..." (Ps. 50:7).

[8] Scriptures clearly depict worship following judgment in Revelation 4, 5, and 19.

1

The Court of Heaven

That God convenes a court in heaven to consider legal issues should not surprise us. As the Great Lawgiver and Judge, God logically presides over an assembly of His creatures and renders righteous judgment.[9] Moreover, God, as a rational and moral being, relates to humankind in a manner that entails reason, evidence, dispute, and persuasion. Since He makes the final decisions and renders justice and judgment, any such assembly should rightly be called a legal court. In addition, any of His reasoned contentions logically take on court terminology, e.g. lawsuits and verdicts. The Bible contains numerous examples of such legal terminology, several of which we will discuss in this study.

Court Council

Not surprisingly, God includes council members in the adjudication process. The Bible calls them "God's council" (Job 15:8; Jer. 23:18, 22) or "the great assembly" (Ps. 82:1; Is. 14:13). The courtroom counselors take the titles of "holy ones"[10] or "watchmen" (Da. 4:13, 23), who apparently observe the deliberations and participate in the discussions.

This council may consist largely of angels, since we find the angel Gabriel acting as a court interpreter, when, for example, he explains the meaning of visions and decrees of the court to Daniel.[11] Angels may also fulfill the roles of court investigators, petitioners, and advocates or as general messengers of court decrees.[12] Zechariah, for one, had a vision of such activity:

> During the night I had a vision—and there before me was a man riding a red horse! He was standing among the myrtle trees in a ravine. Behind him were red, brown and white horses. I asked, "What are these, my lord?" The angel who was talking with me answered, "I will show you what they are." Then the man standing among the myrtle trees explained, "They are the ones the LORD has sent to go throughout the earth." And they reported to the angel of the LORD, who was standing among the myrtle trees, "We have gone throughout the earth and found the whole world at rest and in peace."—Zech. 1:8-11

In this example, God sent angelic horsemen as

His representatives—probably as part of the Divine Court ministry—to examine the evidence of man's actions and state. Their investigation results in mercy and judgments,[13] including deliverance for Joshua, the high priest, from the accusations of Satan (Zech. 3:1-7). The decree of the court follows in the form of a large, flying scroll containing judgments on ungodliness (Zech. 5:1-4). Throughout the entire process, an angel interprets the events for Zechariah.[14]

The twenty-four elders of Revelation's court scene (Rev. 4-5) may also be council participants since they respond with worship to the judgments of God and explain the court actions to John.[15] The issue on the docket before this council concerned finding someone to break the seals of the scroll of judgments (Rev. 5:2). None was found to open the scroll and its seven seals until the Lion/Lamb of God—the Son of God—"came and took the scroll from the right hand of him who sat on the throne" (Rev. 5:7).

Prophets as Court Messengers and Witnesses

Not only do we have permanent residents of heaven and members of the council, but also prophets visit the court of heaven. They witness the proceedings of the Divine Court and are commissioned as messengers of God to deliver the judgments of the court.[16] R. B. Y. Scott commented:

> The prophet was permitted to overhear what went on in the divine council, when Yahweh's word was sent forth to accomplish his purpose in the earth...He was at

the same time Yahweh's witness in his controversy with Israel, and Israel's conscience.[17]

For example, in 1 Kings 22 the prophet Micaiah related his vision of the heavenly court scene to the kings of Judah and Israel:

> Micaiah continued, "Therefore hear the word of the LORD: I saw the LORD sitting on his throne with all the host of heaven standing around him on his right and on his left. And the LORD said, 'Who will entice Ahab into attacking Ramoth Gilead and going to his death there?' One suggested this, and another that. Finally, a spirit came forward, stood before the LORD and said, 'I will entice him.' 'By what means?' the LORD asked. 'I will go out and be a lying spirit in the mouths of all his prophets,' he said. 'You will succeed in enticing him,' said the LORD. 'Go and do it.' So now the LORD has put a lying spirit in the mouths of all these prophets of yours. The LORD has decreed disaster for you." —1 Kings 22:19-23

The background to this scene is as follows. Micaiah son of Imlah was a prophet of Israel during the reigns of King Ahab of Israel and King Jehoshaphat of Judah. Ahab desired to make an alliance with Jehoshaphat to recapture Ramoth Gilead from Aram (Assyria). Before they attacked, the kings wanted assurance of victory through the affirmation of their prophets. Four hundred (false) prophets from Israel prophesied the success of the attack and guaranteed victory. However, Jehoshaphat remained unconvinced and sought a prophet from Jehovah. Reluctantly, Ahab called Micaiah, who prophesied disaster for the armies of Israel and Judah.

I believe Ahab's reluctance to call on Micaiah betrayed his trust in his armies and in his new alliance with Judah more than the word of a multitude of prophets. Ahab most likely intended to use the spectacle of four hundred prophets as a ploy to convince Jehoshaphat to attack Aram. Nevertheless, the prophetic word of Micaiah would spoil his show.

How does this apply to us? As Christians, we need to discern between an exhibition and a true encounter with God, especially in the prophetic realm, where all kinds of abuses have occurred.

In addition, I believe this passage depicts a Divine Court session with the Lord on His throne and the council members surrounding Him. God had already decreed destruction for Ahab and his armies. The issue now before the court concerned the way that destruction would occur. Discussion of the issue resulted in the selection of a lying spirit-messenger to cause the prophets to prophesy falsely and thereby entice the armies to go to war. Micaiah acted as a witness of the court to declare the true verdict to the kings of Israel and Judah.

The vision of the Divine Court is not an isolated one among prophets. Jeremiah expected prophets to speak out of their experience with the council of heaven:

> This is what the LORD Almighty says: "Do not listen to what the prophets are prophesying to you; they fill you with false hopes. They speak visions from their own minds, not from the mouth of the LORD...*But which of them has stood in the council of the LORD to see or to hear his word?* Who has listened and heard his word?
> —Jer. 23:16, 18[18] [emphasis added]

In addition to observing the council, we should note the reason prophets visited heaven: "to see and hear his words." God reveals His heavenly actions through both speech and vision. God often combines words and vivid pictures and symbols to portray His judgments—sometimes illustrated in dramatic form.[19] In similar ways, the prophet may act out God's judgments before His people. When God commissioned Ezekiel, for instance, He gave the prophet a vision of God's portable throne over Jerusalem (Ezek. 1-3):

> Above the expanse over their heads was what looked like a throne of sapphire, and high above on the throne was a figure like that of a man. I saw that from what appeared to be his waist up he looked like glowing metal, as if full of fire, and that

from there down he looked like fire; and brilliant light surrounded him. Like the appearance of a rainbow in the clouds on a rainy day, so was the radiance around him. This was the appearance of the likeness of the glory of the LORD.

—Ezekiel 1:26-28a

God was about to render judgment on the nation and selected Ezekiel to be the bearer of bad tidings. Most likely this passage shows the court of heaven since Ezekiel had to consume the court edicts (Ezek. 2:9-3:4)[20] and then speak and dramatize the impending judgments to the nation (Ezek. 5-6). God's arrival over the temple may be part of a fourteen-month court investigation (Ezek. 5:5; 8:6-18; 9:9) that ended in judgment and the departure of God's glory (Ezek. 10:18; 11:22-23).

These passages show that judgment on earth was first decided in heaven and illustrated there before taking place on earth. Look at a similar example in the opening chapters of Ezekiel. Here a voice from heaven called six executioners to carry out the judgments of the court. A court recorder took an inkhorn and placed the Hebrew letter "tau" on the foreheads of the righteous in the city to prevent them from suffering the same fate as the wicked.[21] Then God symbolized His judgments by casting burning coals over the city (Ezek. 1:13; 10:2). All of this was done in the spiritual realm first, before being accomplished through physical means.

Like the prophets Daniel, Micaiah, and Ezekiel,

Isaiah became a representative of the court to proclaim its resolutions. During Isaiah's vision of heaven, the issue before the court was the selection of a messenger: "Whom shall I send? And who will go for us?" (Is. 6:8a) were the questions posed by the Judge to the council (note the plural form of the latter question). Isaiah gave a prompt reply: "Here am I. Send me!" (Is. 6:8b). As a result, the court commissioned Isaiah to pronounce judgment until "the land is utterly forsaken" (Is. 6:12) and only a remnant remains (Is. 6:13).[22]

Prophets maintained a significant role as messengers of the Divine Court. They frequently brought lawsuits from the Divine Court to Israel[23] or challenged the Israelites to argue their case before the Divine Court:[24]

> Hear the word of the LORD, you Israelites, because the LORD has a charge to bring against you who live in the land: "There is no faithfulness, no love, no acknowledgment of God in the land...
> —Hos. 4:1

> The LORD takes his place in court; he rises to judge the people. The LORD enters into judgment against the elders and leaders of his people... —Is. 3:13-14a

> Review the past for me, let us argue the matter together; state the case for your innocence. —Is. 43:26

As messengers, prophets pronounce to the world what they witness in heaven. This becomes the "testimony" of the Divine Court:

> He commanded us to preach to the people and to testify that he is the one whom God appointed as judge of the living and the dead. All the prophets testify about him that everyone who believes in him receives forgiveness of sins through his name.
> —Acts 10:42-43

We must understand that the term "testimony" is primarily a legal term and part of courtroom drama.[25] Reimer Faber commented on these verses from Acts:

> It has been observed that the motif of legal witness is found throughout [Acts], and that Luke has a penchant to use legal language for theological reasons…When Peter says that the prophets bore witness to the fact that Jesus Christ "is the one ordained by God to be judge of the living and the dead" (v. 42), he makes explicit the legal ramifications of his message.[26]

Christians tend to use the term "testimony" loosely—usually taking it to mean "to share with others what God has personally done for me." While this is certainly a worthy avocation, such usage loses its primary legal connotations. When prophets (and

Christians) witness, they give the legal testimony of the court of heaven. An angel affirmed this to the apostle John: "For the testimony of Jesus is the spirit of prophecy" (Rev. 19:10).

John fulfilled the role of prophet/messenger in Revelation. A voice from heaven invited John through a "door standing open in heaven" (Rev. 4:1) to witness and record the judgments of the court.[27] (Thus he acts as a commissioned prophet.) Again, a voice from heaven instructed him to eat the testimony scroll and then prophesy "about many peoples, nations, languages and kings" (Rev. 10:11). It is no wonder, then, that Scripture refers to the Book of Revelation as prophecy[28] and as the testimony of Christ.[29] The two ideas are synonymous when seen as part of heavenly courtroom drama.

Craig Keener commented:

> "Witness" was especially a legal term, although the sense had been widely extended beyond that. Christians were being betrayed to Roman law courts, but in the context of Revelation, "witness" is the Christian proclamation of knowledge about Jesus, providing evidence in light of the court of God's final judgment (cf. Is. 43:8-12; 44:8-9).[30]

The testimony prophets speak is the truth evaluation that Christ has made regarding all things. It is based on His righteous nature and acts—especially His redemptive acts. It should be obvious, then, that the gospel largely makes up the testimony of Christ,[31] which originates from heaven,[32] is itself called a "witness" (Mt. 24:14), and is based on a verdict of the court:

> Whoever believes in him is not condemned, but whoever does not believe stands condemned already because he has not believed in the name of God's one and only Son. This is the verdict: Light has come into the world, but men loved darkness instead of light because their deeds were evil. —Jn. 3:18-19

Thus, prophets declare the testimony of the Divine Court to the world, convicting the world and bringing it in line with the will of the Judge. The whole essence of prophecy comes from understanding what happens in heaven as a result of Christ's testimony. This includes present court actions and future judgments.

Christ as Court Advocate

Job identified an arbiter, witness, and vindicator/redeemer[33] who represented him to the Divine Court against the accusations of Satan. This advocate represented Job not as an attorney to a client, which we see in courtrooms today, but as a close friend and confidant.[34] Job explained:

> Even now my witness is in heaven; my advocate is on high. My intercessor is my

friend as my eyes pour out tears to God; on behalf of a man he pleads with God as a man pleads for his friend.

—Job 16:19-21

Most likely Job's representative is none other than the Son of God,[35] whom the Bible identifies as our advocate (1 Jn. 2:1), the Faithful and True Witness,[36] our Intercessor (Ro. 8:34; He. 7:25), and the "Amen" (the final word in court; Is. 65:16; 2 Cor. 1:20). As our advocate, Christ pleads our cause with the Father, reconciles us to Him, and secures the grace and mercy we need to face the problems of life.[37]

Since Christ knows the Father intimately and since Christ fulfilled the legal requirements to bring us back into relationship with the Father, Christ is the consummate advocate for our defense. Christ's redemption makes up for our fatal deficiency and becomes the basis for all arguments on our behalf:

My dear children, I write this to you so that you will not sin. But if anybody does sin, we have one who speaks to the Father in our defense—Jesus Christ, the Righteous One. He is the atoning sacrifice for our sins, and not only for ours but also for the sins of the whole world.

—1 Jn. 2:1-2

Who will bring any charge against those whom God has chosen? It is God who justifies. Who is he that condemns? Christ

> Jesus, who died—more than that, who was
> raised to life—is at the right hand of God
> and is also interceding for us.
>
> —Ro. 8:33-34

Thus, no other representative can plead our case before the Judge in heaven from the same legal ground.

In Biblical times the advocate was the kinsman-redeemer who would represent a relative in legal cases.[38] As our near kinsman-redeemer, Christ understands our situation completely. In this role, which overlaps with his role as High Priest, Christ intercedes for us with great empathy and compassion according to our needs (cf. Lk. 22:31-32; Jn. 17:9, 15). Without Christ's roles as mediator, intercessor, and advocate, we would merit severe judgments from the Divine Court. We can rejoice, however, that from heaven Christ continues to minister, interceding on behalf of the Church.

From the example of Israel's priests, Joel may give us a glimpse of Christ's compassionate heart as He intercedes for us:

> Let the priests, who minister before the
> LORD, weep between the temple porch
> and the altar. Let them say, "Spare your
> people, O LORD. Do not make your inher-
> itance an object of scorn, a byword among
> the nations. Why should they say among
> the peoples, 'Where is their God?'" Then

the LORD will be jealous for his land and
take pity on his people.—Joel 2:17-18

Christ interceded for both His immediate and
future disciples (Lk. 22:32; Jn. 17) and even for
those who crucified Him (Lk. 23:34). Christ Himself
spoke of His future advocacy role in heaven:

> Whoever acknowledges me before men, I
> will also acknowledge him before my
> Father in heaven. But whoever disowns me
> before men, I will disown him before my
> Father in heaven. —Mt. 10:32-33

Since Christ has opened up a way for us into the
heavenlies (He. 9:11-12; 24-26; 10:19-22), and since
He has offered His blood there, then we have the
legal right to present our cases to the court of heaven.
This privilege cannot be overemphasized, but we
will examine this further in Chapter 4.

Christ as Court Prophet and Witness

Like all prophets, Christ fulfills the role of messenger for the Divine Court, except that Christ is *the
Prophet* who was sent from heaven with the testimony of God the Judge (Deut. 18:18-19; Jn. 8:12-18,
50; cf. Mal. 3:1-5).[39] During His earthly ministry
Christ spoke prophetically in the usual sense of pre-
dicting the future,[40] but He also spoke as a prophet
keenly aware of His connection to heaven—in many
cases using courtroom language of "witness" and
"testimony:"

Jesus answered, "Even if I testify on my
own behalf, my testimony is valid, for I
know where I came from and where I am
going. But you have no idea where I come
from or where I am going...In your own
Law it is written that the testimony of two
men is valid. I am one who testifies for
myself; my other witness is the Father,
who sent me."

—Jn. 8:14, 17-18[41]

The one who comes from heaven is above
all. He testifies to what he has seen and
heard, but no one accepts his testimony.

—Jn. 3:31b-32

While Christ may refer to His own works in this
last verse (cf. 1 Jn. 1:2-3), He may also allude to
Jeremiah 23 to show how He fulfills the requirement
of "seeing and hearing" from heaven's council. In
any case, Christ was a witness of heaven's decisions.
He was perfectly united to the Judge and submitted
to His decisions.

During Peter's speech at Pentecost, Luke correlates Christ the Prophet to God's legal representative
by showing that those who reject the Prophet come
under severe condemnation from the Judge:

For Moses said, "The Lord your God will
raise up for you a prophet like me from
among your own people; you must listen
to everything he tells you. Anyone who

does not listen to him will be completely cut off from among his people."
—Acts 3:22-23 (cf. Acts 7:37)

Peter quotes from Deuteronomy 18:15-19 where God clearly states, "If anyone does not listen to my words that the prophet speaks in my name, I myself will call him to account." To "call to account" is legal terminology of the court (Mt. 12:36-37).[42]

In a similar way, Christ's prophetic "woes" pronounced against cities (Mt. 11:21), against those who bring offence (Mt. 18:7), and against the teachers of the law and Pharisees (Mt. 23:13ff) were legal judgments much the same as the "woes" pronounced by Old Testament prophets. All reveal Christ's connection to the Divine Court.

Christ further demonstrated His connection to heaven through His intimate fellowship with the Father. For instance, the words that the Father gave, the Son gave to others (Jn. 7:16-17; 8:40, 47; 12:49-50), as the Father worked, so did the Son (Jn. 5:17-19), and *the Son spoke what He has seen in the Father's presence* (Jn. 8:38). Conversely, the Father always heard the Son (Jn. 11:42). Christ declared: "For I have come down from heaven not to do my will but to do the will of him who sent me" (Jn. 6:38) and again, "…for this reason I was born, and for this I came into the world, to testify to the truth" (Jn. 18:37). Thus, Christ was heaven's perfect *Witness*.

The significance of these phrases should not be overlooked. Everything Christ did as His mission was vitally linked to heaven (Jn. 8:42). Christ's testimony about His life thoroughly incorporates the direction of His heavenly Father. Thus, to say that Christian witnessing involves only reciting the Christ event fails to take into account our connection with heaven. Therefore, to witness also means to give testimony under the direction of the Judge.

That Christ is the Witness of heaven's court can be seen also from His title as "Faithful and True Witness."[43] As the pre-eminent official of the divine council and as the special representative of the court, Christ's mission while on earth was to bear witness to covenant truth. Christ's light shone forth as a witness that exposed the evil deeds of the world. The world hated Christ because He testified that "what it does is evil" (Jn. 7:7). Christ stood for truth (Jn. 18:37) in the face of persecution and suffering. He was a faithful witness even to death.

The testimony of Christ was rejected by the world (Jn. 12:47-49), but vindicated by His resurrection (Ro. 1:4; Acts 2:22-36; Eph. 1:20-23), and commended to the seven churches (Rev. 2-3). His prophetic testimony contains the truth of righteous judgment to come (Rev. 19:10-11) and His words will condemn unbelievers on the last day (Jn. 12:48).

The Holy Spirit as Court Advocate

The Bible uses the word "Paraclete" to denote Christ as our advocate (1 John 2:1). In John 14:16, Christ promised another advocate, the Holy Spirit, to be with us forever. (We should note, as many commentators point out, that the Greek word for "another" means "another of the same kind.") D. A.

Carson explained the meaning of the Greek word translated "advocate:"

> "Parakletos primarily means 'legal assistant, advocate,' someone who helps another in court, whether as an advocate, a witness, or a representative...the Paraklete serves rather more as a prosecuting attorney than as counsel for the defense. 'Counselor' is not wrong, so long as 'legal counselor' is understood, not 'camp counselor' or 'marriage counselor.' "[44]

Carson is correct in highlighting the legal aspects of "paraklete," but we should recognize that the role of advocate might be twofold: to *defend* and to *prosecute*.[45] While the Holy Spirit's role is largely that of prosecution, Christ's advocacy ministry is primarily for our defense.[46] We have already seen that Christ intercedes on our behalf in the Court of heaven. To intercede means at least partly that Christ defends us to the Father.

In contrast, the Holy Spirit prosecutes the case for Christ against the world. In other words, as we speak the gospel testimony, the Holy Spirit guides us and, in fact, personally testifies through us (1 Jn. 5:6; cf. Mt. 10:16-20). A. A. Trites commented on the earthly advocacy role:

> While he was on earth, Jesus bore witness to the truth and served as the chief advocate for God in the world (18:37; 10:34-38;

14:10-11; 18:23). Now his juridical functions are taken over by "another Paraclete,"
the Holy Spirit promised by Jesus
(14:16–18).[47]

The Holy Spirit convicts "the world of guilt in
regard to sin and righteousness and judgment" (Jn.
16:8). To "convict" (elencho) is to prove legally
guilty. Again, John uses "legal terminology for the
trial."[48] This Greek word may include all three legal
aspects of making God's case: to investigate,
expose, and convict. In John 8:46 Christ used the
term with these aspects: "Can any of you *prove me
guilty* of sin?"

First of all, the Holy Spirit exposes and convicts
the world of sin, because the world refuses to believe
in Christ; secondly of righteousness, because
Christ's ascension vindicated His testimony as righteous; and lastly of judgment, because those who
reject Christ and follow Satan are condemned with
him. The Holy Spirit "substantiates our witness" [49]
as He points His divine finger at the hearts of the
unrighteous and says, "you are guilty." Further, He
convinces unbelievers that Satan "now stands condemned" (Jn. 16:11).

Just as it would be necessary for the evidence in
a trial to be truthful to bring any authentic, convicting effect, so the advocacy ministry of the Holy
Spirit must be grounded in the truth. To this end,
Christ described the Spirit as "the Spirit of Truth"
(Jn. 14:17; 15:26; 16:13) who "will guide you into
all truth" (Jn. 16:13). Similarly, for our witness to

carry any weight in the courts of men's hearts, we must bear testimony based on the Spirit's revealed truth—both objective truth, based on Scripture, and subjective truth, based on the present revelation of the Holy Spirit.

In this role, then, the Holy Spirit acts as a joint *witness* with us (Jn. 15:26-27; Acts 1:8; 1 Jn. 5:6-9), testifying on behalf of Christ and enabling us to testify aligned with Christ's truth. (In a related sense, Paul spoke of the Holy Spirit as the one who "testifies with our spirit that we are God's children" [Ro. 8:16].)

Another example of the Holy Spirit's role as our advocate occurs in Matthew 10:19-20 (cf., Mk. 13:11). If unbelievers unjustly prosecute Christians before their courts (which supposedly represent God, cf. Ps. 82), the Holy Spirit will immediately prompt the Christians with what to say. This strongly suggests that the Holy Spirit supernaturally communicates with us as we represent Christ as witnesses to this world. In this regard, *I believe the gifts of the Spirit are the necessary tools through which the will of heaven's court reaches earth.*

Christ specifically tied prophecy to the advocacy ministry of the Holy Spirit:

> But I tell you the truth: It is for your good that I am going away. Unless I go away, the Counselor [Advocate] will not come to you; but if I go, I will send him to you...But when he, the Spirit of truth, comes, he will guide you into all truth. He will not speak on his own; he will speak

only what he hears, and *he will tell you what is yet to come.*
>   —Jn. 16:7, 13 [emphasis mine]

Paul confirms this in his epistle to the Corinthians:

> But if an unbeliever or someone who does not understand comes in while everybody is prophesying, he will be convinced by all that he is a sinner and will be judged by all, and the secrets of his heart will be laid bare. So he will fall down and worship God, exclaiming, "God is really among you!"
>   —1 Cor. 14:24-25

I believe Paul had the Spirit's advocacy role also in mind when he explained that speaking in tongues is a sign to unbelievers of God's impending judgment:

> In the Law it is written: "Through men of strange tongues and through the lips of foreigners I will speak to this people, but even then they will not listen to me," says the Lord. Tongues, then, are a sign, not for believers but for unbelievers…
>   —1 Cor. 14:21-22a

In these verses, Paul quotes from Isaiah 28 where God's sign of judgment would be the foreign tongues of Israel's invaders. This is one of the remarkable purposes for tongues not often mentioned today. (By this I don't mean that we have invaders coming, but that unbelievers are under His judgment already.) The fact that Christians speak in tongues is a sign to unbelievers of God's verdict. The gifts are, in effect, vehicles for delivering God's legal actions and messages.

Even though the Holy Spirit is our resident advocate, He still appeals to the Judge on our behalf:

> In the same way, the Spirit helps us in our weakness. We do not know what we ought to pray for, but the Spirit himself intercedes for us with groans that words cannot express. And he who searches our hearts knows the mind of the Spirit, because the Spirit intercedes for the saints in accordance with God's will. —Ro. 8:26

All believers, including New Testament prophets, receive directly from the heavenly intercessory ministry of Christ via the presence of the Council Advocate—or Holy Spirit—within us.[50] In addition, we all have access to the heavenlies (including the Divine Council) through our connection to Christ, who is the Head of the Body and our advocate in heaven.[51]

Prayer is the means by which God brings about this connection. Through prayer, God communicates His will via words of knowledge and wisdom, and through prophecy.

We have then an advocate within us and an advocate in the heavenlies. This two-way connectedness makes us well-suited witnesses to accomplish God's will on earth. The Council Advocate, or Holy Spirit, is in us testifying through us and convicting the world (Jn. 14:15-17; 16:7-15). The Holy Spirit now takes of the Lord's ministry in heaven and makes it known to members of the Church and through them to the world.

All believers, though especially New Testament prophets, must remain keenly aware of the Divine Council and Christ's current ministry. Christians must know and declare Christ's testimony, including His evaluations of the Church.[52]

Court Accuser

We have already seen that Satan accused both Job and Joshua the high priest in Old Testament accounts.[53] Revelation also indicates that Satan accuses brothers "day and night" in heaven before being cast down (Rev. 12:10). In fact, the Hebrew word for Satan means "accuser." (He is also known for rebellion, lying, slandering, deceiving, and inciting evil.)[54] In Luke 22:32 we find Jesus explaining that Satan "asked to sift" Peter as wheat, but Christ, acting as Peter's advocate, countered with the petition that his faith not fail.

Despite Satan's temptations, Christ always acted in perfect obedience to the Father and refused to succumb to Satan's schemes. Satan desired legal authority over Christ, but never achieved any:

> I will not speak with you much longer, for the prince of this world is coming. He has no hold on me... —Jn. 14:30

This verse shows that no accusation can be made against Christ—Satan has no legal hold on or lien against Him (Jn. 14:30). D. A. Carson commented, *"He has no hold on me* is an idiomatic rendering of 'he has nothing in me', recalling a Hebrew idiom frequently used in legal contexts..."[55]

Christ's redemption and our subsequent justification cancelled our legal debt to sin (Col. 2:14). Satan lost his case against humankind at the cross. He stands condemned and therefore forfeits his legal claim over humankind. Consequently, Satan can no longer make an accusation against us with any authority. The legal indictments[56] against us no longer have merit:

> Who will bring any charge against those whom God has chosen? It is God who justifies. Who is he that condemns? Christ Jesus, who died—more than that, who was raised to life—is at the right hand of God and is also interceding for us.
>
> —Ro. 8:33-34

While some contend that Satan continues to accuse us before the Father, much as he did with Job, the Scriptures most likely portray the ejection of Satan from heaven's courtroom—never to return—after the ascension of Christ and the final cleansing of heaven (He. 9:23; cf. He. 8:3-6). It seems hardly likely that heaven should be cleansed and yet have the most unclean thing—Satan—continue to have the right to work his intrigues there.

One's view of this largely derives from a few passages in the Gospels and from Revelation 12:7-17. Since Revelation contains numerous symbols and literary forms, numerous interpretations of the book abound. Consequently, we should start with the verses from the Gospels and then proceed to the more difficult passage in Revelation. In all cases, gracious tolerance for different opinions should guide us.

Following the victory of the apostles over Satan's demons, Christ recounted a vision of Satan's sudden and violent fall from heaven as lightning:

> He replied, "I saw Satan fall like lightning from heaven. I have given you authority to trample on snakes and scorpions and to overcome all the power of the enemy; nothing will harm you. However, do not rejoice that the spirits submit to you, but rejoice that your names are written in heaven."
>
> —Lk. 10:18-20

This verse pinpoints one of Satan's falls from heaven. The statement is probably an actual sighting since "vision" here refers most often to physical sight and is not the Greek word for "prophetic vision."[57] This verse does reveal that the victory over Satan on earth by the disciples results in his expulsion from heaven, at least temporarily. In other words, the in-breaking of the Kingdom of Heaven on earth resulted in a fall of Satan from heaven.

In John 12:29-33, Christ seems to link His victory over death to the moment when Satan is driven out:

Jesus said, "This voice was for your benefit, not mine. Now is the time for judgment
on this world; now the prince of this world
will be driven out. But I, when I am lifted
up from the earth, will draw all men to
myself." He said this to show the kind of
death he was going to die. —Jn. 12:29-33

The contrast seems to show that by the "lifting
up" of Christ, Satan was "cast out." Neither passage
leaves us with absolute certainty as to the timing of
Satan's final removal and the latter one does not
show us the location from which Satan is removed.
Hebrews may tip the scales in favor of Satan's final
expulsion after Christ's resurrection and ascension
(see above), but Revelation 12 offers the most defini-
tive scenario of Satan's final removal from heaven:

Then I heard a loud voice in heaven say:
"Now have come the salvation and the
power and the kingdom of our God, and
the authority of his Christ. For the accuser
of our brothers, who accuses them before
our God day and night, has been hurled
down."—Rev. 12:10[58]

I believe this interlude residing in Revelation 12-
14 gives a summary of testimony in the manner of a
vision/drama, much the same as Ezekiel's dramati-
zations (Ezek. 4-5). The summary in Revelation contains a series of events—both past and future—
portrayed in seven vignettes or "seven signs" that

forms the legal testimony exhibited before the court.[59] This testimony becomes the basis for dispensing judgments against Satan and his kingdom.[60]

In addition, the fact that the male child (vs. 5) rules the "nations with an iron scepter" is such an obvious reference to Christ that none other should be sought.[61] The glorious woman (vs. 1-2, 6, and 13) most likely represents the Messianic Community from which is birthed Christ and the Church. The rebellion in heaven, the rescue/ascension of Christ, war in heaven, and the casting out of Satan from heaven (vs. 4-5, 7-12) are past events. This correlates best with the accounts in the Gospels. The three and a half year period, first mentioned in verse 6 and then picked up again by the narrative in verses 14 forward, refers to the future.

As a result of being cast from heaven, God has limited Satan's sphere of operation to the first and second heavens. He no longer has access to the third heaven—the heaven of God's throne. Thus, Satan no longer accuses us in the court of heaven. Heaven has been permanently cleansed!

The Judge

Presiding over the court from His exalted throne, the Father renders judgments on matters great and small according to the awesome integrity of His nature.[62] In fact, having no greater to swear by, the Lord has sworn by Himself (Amos 4:2; 6:8; He. 6:16-17; 7:20-21). Taking an oath was a legal action offered as validation of a matter before the court (Ex. 22:10-13; Ps. 50:1-4).[63] Justice and mercy hallmark

His decisions and on the basis of these, humankind petitions the Lord (Is. 64:8-12).

Lest we think God is far removed from us, however, we should remember God's personal investigations of Sodom and Gomorrah (Ge. 18:20-21), or His portable throne over the temple in Jerusalem (Ezek. 1-10). The prophet Malachi declared that on the Day of His coming God will "come near to you for judgment" and will testify against evil doers (Mal. 3:1-6). God is the God who comes. He may be "high above on the throne" (Ezek. 1:26), but He is also close and personal (Ps. 139).

Isaiah declared that "The LORD is our Judge" (Is. 33:22) for He is the one who "has pronounced sentence"[64] (Is. 34:2) on the people. None will escape His Great White Throne—and not everyone will escape His wrath (Ge. 18:25; Ro. 2:5; 1 Thess. 1:10; Rev. 20:11-15). To those who reject Christ, the Judge has already pronounced them guilty. To those who have received Christ's atonement, the Judge pronounces a verdict in their favor—"even life forevermore" (Ps. 133:3).

Though the Father is the Judge of all humankind, He has elected to give all judgment to the Son.[65] In this sense, Christ too is Judge (Acts 10:42). The apostle John expressed this with a sense of joint courtroom ministry between the Father and Son (Jn. 8:14-18; 12:44-50). The testimony of the Son combines with the testimony of the Father to establish truth. Similarly, the Son judges based on the authority given to Him from the Father. They stand together as joint advocates: "But if I do judge, my decisions are right, because I am not alone. I stand with the Father, who sent me" (Jn. 8:16).

ENDNOTES

[9] Ps. 7:11; 76:9; 96:10-13; Is. 3:13; 33:22; Ro. 2:16; 2 Tim. 4:1; He. 10:30; 12:23; Ja. 4:12; Rev. 20:11-15.

[10] Ex. 24:9-10; Job 15:8; Ps. 82:1; 89:5, 7.

[11] Da. 8:15; 9:21ff; cf. Lk. 1:19.

[12] Investigators - Zech. 1:8-11; petitioners - Zech. 1:12-13; advocates - Job. 33:23-24; messengers - Zech. 3:1-10; Rev. 1:1-3; 2:1, 8, et. al.; 10:1-4; 22:6.

[13] See Zech. 1-6.

[14] Zech. 1:14-20; 4:1-7, 11-14; 5:1-11; 6:1-8.

[15] Rev. 5:5-10, 14; 7:11-17; 11:16-18; 14:3; 19:4.

[16] Is. 41:27; Jer. 23:18; Is. 3:13-15, 25-26; 6:8; 41:27; Ezek. 2-3 (especially 2:9-3:1); Amos 3:7; Hag. 1:13; Mal. 3:1; Rev. 4:1; 11:3-12; 22:18-19.

[17] R. B. Y. Scott, *Priesthood, Prophecy, Wisdom and the Knowledge of God*, **Journal of Biblical Literature**, 80 (1961) 9-10.

[18] Note that the NIV has "council" not "counsel" as the AV. See also Is. 6:8 and Amos 3:7.

[19] See, for example, Nu. 24:15-17; Zech. 5:5-11; and Rev. 12-14.

[20] An opisthograph scroll (written on both sides; cf. Rev. 5:1).

[21] As the last letter of the Hebrew alphabet, this may represent the remnant.

[22] See also Jn. 12:39-41.

[23] Is. 1:2-3, 18-20; 3:13-15, 25-26; Lam. 3:58; Ho. 3:3-17; 4:1-19; Amos 3:1; Micah 6:1-5. See also Rev. 6:10. A prophet's authority rested squarely on knowing the will of the court and in the confidence that God would back up His decisions (Is. 44:26).

[24] Is. 41:21-23; 43:26; see also Job 19:25; Jer. 12:1; Prov. 23:10-11.

[25] See Deuteronomy 19:15-19 and John 8:17; Mark 14:56-63, Acts 7:57-58, etc. Also see William Arndt and Wilbur Gingrich, translators, Walter Bauer, *A Greek-English Lexicon of the New Testament and Other Early Christian Literature* (Chicago: University Press, 1974) 494-495.

[26] Riemer Faber, *The Juridical Nuance in the NT Use of Προσωπολημψια*, **Westminster Theological Journal**, vol. 57, no. 2, (Fall 1995) 303.

[27] The court convenes in Rev. 4-5; 9:13; and 20. Revelation records judgments throughout the book.

[28] Rev. 19:10; 22:7, 10, 18-19.

[29] Rev. 1:2, 9; 12:17; 19:10 (2x); 20:4.

[30] Keener, 764.

[31] See especially 1 Cor. 1:6; 2:1; 1 Tim. 2:6; 2 Tim. 1:8; 2 Thess. 1:10; and 1 Jn. 5:11-12.

[32] Mt. 13:35; Jn. 3:31-34; Eph. 1:4; 1 Pt. 1:20ff; Rev. 13:8; 17:8.

[33] Job 9:33; 16:19-21; 19:25-27. The Hebrew "go'el" (redeemer) is used in OT jurisprudence.

[34] G. G. Findlay concurs: "The relationship of advocate and client constituted a settled personal tie involving acquaintance-ship, and often kinship, between the parties. The παράκλητος of the old jurisprudence, in the best times of antiquity, was no hired pleader connected with his client for the occasion by his brief and his fee; he was his patron and standing counsel, the head of the order or the clan to which both belonged, bound by

the claims of honour and family association to stand by his humble dependent and to see him through when his legal standing was imperiled; he was his client's natural protector and the appointed captain of his salvation." Cited in Walt Russel, *The Holy Spirit's Ministry in the Fourth Gospel*, **Grace Theological Journal**, vol. 8, no. 2, Fall 1987, 235. See G. G. Findlay, *The Fellowship in Life Eternal* (New York: Hodder and Stoughton, 1909; reprint ed.; Minneapolis: James and Klock, 1977) 117.

[35] Though Job may not have known that Christ was his advocate.

[36] Rev. 5:6, 8, 11-13; 6:1; 7:17; 21:22-23.

[37] See Lk. 22:31-32 and Jn. 17:9, 15, and 20.

[38] See Lev. 25:25-34; 48-52; Nu. 35:19; Ruth 2:20; 3:9, 13; 4:1-14; Prov. 23:11; Job 19:25; and Jer. 50:34. God was Israel's redeemer/advocate for the Exodus (Ps. 19:14; 78:35; Is. 49:26; 63:16). The Hebrew is "go'el."

[39] See Mt. 13:57; Lk. 13:33; Jn. 4:19; 6:14; 7:40; 9:17; He. 1:1-2. For an excellent summary of Christ as the Prophet, see TDNT, vol. 3, pp. 842ff.

[40] See Mt. 17:22-23; 24-25; and Jn. 13:18-19.

[41] Note that the Father is also a witness; cf. Jer. 29:23; Micah 1:2.

[42] See Josh. 22:23; 1 Sa. 20:16; 2 Chron. 24:19-22; Eccl. 3:15; Ps. 10:13, 15; and Amos 3:2, 14. The NIV sometimes has "punish" for call to account (Ex. 20:5; Jer. 5:9, 29; Hos. 1:4). See Shalom Paul, *Amos: A Commentary on the Book of Amos* (Minneapolis: Fortress Press, 1991).

[43] Rev. 1:5; 3:14; 19:11.

[44] D. A. Carson, *The Gospel According to John* (Grand Rapids: William. B. Eerdmans Publishing Co., 1991) 117.

[45] Of course, Carson does not deny that both aspects are part of the meaning of "paraklete," he is simply emphasizing the

meaning as applied to the Holy Spirit.

[46] The Bible calls the Father "Advocate" as well: Isaiah 50:7-9; Jer 50:34; 51:36; Lam. 3:58–66; Ps 43:1; 50:8.

[47] A. A. Trites, *Witness*, in Joel G.Green, Scot McKnight, I. Howard Marshall, editors, *Dictionary of Jesus and the Gospels* (Downer's Grove, IL: InterVarsity Press, 1998) 879.

[48] Gary Burge, *John*, in Walter Elwell, editor, *Evangelical Commentary on the Bible*, (Grand Rapids: Baker, 1989) 871.

[49] Op. cit.

[50] The Church now has the authority to commission prophets due to the empowerment and authorization of the Holy Spirit. Unlike the experience of many prophets in the Old Testament, it is no longer necessary to have a vision of the Divine Council to be commissioned as a prophet. The Holy Spirit now provides the connection and sanctions and legitimizes the prophetic commission (Jn. 20:21-23; Acts 13:1-3; 20:28). The New Testament prophet is the believer who exercises the gift of prophecy in a seasoned way and is recognized (usually through ordination) by the Church.

[51] Eph. 1:22-23; Col. 1:18; He. 4:16; 7:24; 8:1-2; 1 Jn. 2:1.

[52] See, for instance, John's report to the seven churches of Asia of the messengers from heaven in Revelation 2-3. Although we have dealt with the connection with the Divine Court through the presence of the Advocate within us, Psalm 82 makes explicit the connection between human judges and the Divine Court (at least with appointed judges within the theocracy). So much are these earthly judges considered representatives of God's legal action that the Psalmist calls them "gods." This shows the derived authority of the earthly court and its ultimate responsibility to heaven.

[53] Job 1-2; Zech. 3:1-2. Satan is most likely the candidate though Scripture is not explicit that only one individual is meant.

[54] 1 Chron. 21:1; Is. 14:13-15; Ezek. 28:15-18; 2 Cor. 11:14; 1

Jn. 3:8.

[55] D. A. Carson, *The Gospel According to John*, 508.

[56] τις ἐγκαλέσει κατὰ ἐκλεκτῶν θεοῦ.

[57] See θεωρεώ in W. F. Arndt and F. W. Gingrich, *A Greek-English Lexicon of the New Testament and Other Early Christian Literature* (Chicago: The University of Chicago Press, 1957) 360. This "vision" is different from an apparition/vision (ὀπτασίαν) in Lk. 1:22; 24:23; Acts 16:19; and 2 Cor. 12:1.

[58] Since this interlude resides in the chapters of Revelation concerning future events (after the opening of the seals), many expositors interpret this entire passage as part of the same flow of future events. However, viewing this passage as an interlude and as a summary of events dramatized in heaven provides a simple explanation for its purpose and position in Revelation without forcing all the events into the future.

[59] The prelude to chapters 12-14 begins in Revelation 11:19 where we see the temple opened in heaven and the Ark of the Covenant revealed. (Elsewhere in Revelation the temple furniture play a role in introducing the next events. See Rev. 1:12, 20; 2:1, 5; 6:9-11; 8:3-5; 9:13-16; 11:4; 11:19; 14:18; 15:1-2, 5-8; 16:1, 17. See also Amos 9:1.) Just as a historical record was kept by the ark as part of the covenant protocol between God and Israel (Josh. 24:25-27; 1 Sa. 10:25) as a testimony against the nation (Deut. 31:26), so this may be the historical summary against Satan. Keeping a copy of the covenant terms between parties was a common practice in covenant making. See M. G. Kline, *Treaty of the Great King* (Grand Rapids: Eerdmans, 1963). See also Harold Stigers, *Preservation, the Corollary of Inspiration*, **Journal of the Evangelical Theological Society**, vol. 22, Sept. 1979, 219. (On a side note, the ruler of God's people made another copy for himself [Deut. 17:18-20].)

[60] It may in fact be the contents of the Lamb's scroll (which was kept by the ark), since all the seals have been broken at this

point. Seals were placed on a scroll to legally authenticate its contents. Only the person who placed the seals was permitted to break them. Therefore, Christ alone could break the seals because He attached them to the scroll. This was His scroll— His testimony.

[61] Ps. 2:9; Rev. 19:15.

[62] Ps. 7:6-8. The Father also fulfills the role of advocate. See 1 Sa. 25:39; Ps. 43:1; Micah 7:9.

[63] In fact, the oath was synonymous with making a covenant— a sworn agreement. See G. M. Tucker, *Covenant Forms and Contract Forms*, VT, 15 (1965), 487-503.

[64] J. B. Phillips, *Four Prophets: A Modern Translation from the Hebrew* (New York: The MacMillan Company, 1963) 137.

[65] Mt. 25:31-46; Lk. 21:36; Jn. 5:22; Acts 10:42.

2

Courtroom Ministry in the Old Testament

Courtroom Proceedings

As we have seen, the Bible often describes the activity and participants of heaven in forensic terms. We should further note that "summons to trial opens the literature of Amos, Micah, Isaiah and Jeremiah."[66] We want to now turn our attention to several court cases and the proceedings of the Divine Court, which generally take place along the following lines:

1. The Divine Court convenes to decide the fate of individuals or nations. The members of the court surround the Judge who sits on the throne and presides over the court.[67]

2. The court may also consider an issue or law-suit.[68] For example, the prophets often brought lawsuits against the nations receiving judgment.[69] These lawsuits were based on moral violations and breech of covenant with God. They contain the legal officials, charges, evidence, and verdict of the court case.

In the following example from Isaiah, the prophet declares the covenant lawsuit:

> The LORD takes his place in court; he rises to judge the people. The LORD enters into judgment against the elders and leaders of his people: "It is you who have ruined my vineyard; the plunder from the poor is in your houses. What do you mean by crushing my people and grinding the faces of the poor?" declares the Lord, the LORD Almighty…"Your men will fall by the sword, your warriors in battle. The gates of Zion will lament and mourn; des-titute, she will sit on the ground."
> —Isaiah 3:13-15, 25-26

3. God may direct an investigation of the issues (Ezek. 1-11; Zech. 1:8-11). For example, Christ's messages to the seven churches of Asia (Rev. 2-3), most likely resulted from His examination of each congregation. The seven "golden lampstands" of John's vision repre-sent each church (Rev. 1:12, 20; 2:5). Christ's

walk among the lampstands seems to indicate that He measured each Church's witness based on its radiance. Christ sent His evaluation via a messenger to each of the seven churches (Rev. 1:16; 2:1; etc.) and by prophetic vision to John.[70]

4. Satan accused individuals in the past (Job 1:9, 2:4; Zech. 3:1; Lk. 22:31; Rev. 12:10). Now, as then, an advocate—most probably Jesus Christ—intercedes for our defense[71] or testifies against evil.[72] (Evidently, Christ's current intercession results from our failures rather than from any accusation from Satan [cf. 1 Jn. 1:5-2:1].)

In some cases, prophets acted as mediators and intercessors for the people,[73] staving off severe judgments for sins committed by the nation. The following scene depicts courtroom drama:

This is what the Sovereign LORD showed me: He was preparing swarms of locusts after the king's share had been harvested and just as the second crop was coming up. When they had stripped the land clean, I cried out, "Sovereign LORD, forgive! How can Jacob survive? He is so small!" So the LORD relented. "This will not happen," the LORD said. —Amos 7:1-3

5. Discussion of the issue(s) before the court

may take place (1 Kings 22:20; Is. 6:8), evidence may be presented from the record books,[74] or testimony may be heard (Micah 1:2; Rev. 6:10). Hosea indicated that God "faithfully records all their evil" (Ho. 7:2).[75]

6. God may apply a standard to the accused. Thus God applied a plumb line to the nation of Israel to "test my people by the straightness of this line"[76] (Amos 7:7-9; cf. Rev. 11:1).

7. The court sits and the Judge stands to render a verdict:[77]

But the court will sit, and his [Antichrist's] power will be taken away and completely destroyed forever. —Da. 7:26

The LORD takes his place in court; he rises to judge the people. —Is. 3:13

8. The court records the verdict, and God may keep it before Him to bring it to pass (Is. 65:6).

9. Impending judgment may be portrayed symbolically or in dramatic form (Amos 8:1-3). For example, a divine "cup" symbolized the accumulation of crimes justly registered by the Divine Court ("piled up to heaven," Rev. 18:5-6)[78] against Babylon and measured back on the guilty. Thus Babylon will

receive a "double portion from her own cup" (Rev. 18:6).[79]

10. The court appoints a messenger or messengers to reveal or carry out the will of the court.[80] For example, God commanded Habakkuk to record his vision so that a messenger may read it:

Then the LORD replied: "Write down the revelation and make it plain on tablets so that a herald may run with it. For the revelation awaits an appointed time; it speaks of the end and will not prove false. Though it linger, wait for it; it will certainly come and will not delay." —Hab. 2:2-3

An indictment follows in verses 4-5, resulting in the verdict of six woes (vs. 6-20) and including the symbol of God's judgment, "the cup of the Lord's right hand" (vs. 16).

(In many cases the Bible is an earthly copy of heavenly court judgments—the prophets having recorded what the Court decides in heaven [Ex. 17:14; Jer. 30:2; 36:2].)

11. The court may set its seal on individuals to show approval or to protect them from judgments. Thus, the Father set His seal of authentication on the testimony of Christ (Jn. 6:27). The angel with "the writing kit at his side" placed a mark of protection on

those in Jerusalem who grieved and lamented over all the "detestable things" done in it (Ezek. 9:3-5). A messenger sealed the 144,000 to preserve their testimony for the court (Rev. 7:3).[81]

12. The court and those who attend the proceedings offer worship to God for His just judgments.[82] Daniel records a vision of a verdict followed by worship:

"In my vision at night I looked, and there before me was one like a son of man, coming with the clouds of heaven. He approached the Ancient of Days and was led into his presence. He was given authority, glory and sovereign power; *all peoples, nations and men of every language worshiped him.* His dominion is an everlasting dominion that will not pass away, and his kingdom is one that will never be destroyed."
—Da. 7:13-14 [emphasis added]

Job's Case Against God

The book of Job moves back and forth between scenes of the Divine Court in heaven and the earthly trial of Job (much the same as movement of scenes in Revelation). The issue before the court was Job's righteousness (Job 1:6-12). We often think of his difficulties as a trial of suffering, but, as David Duel points out, the Hebrew really means a trial as part of the due process of the court. Thus when Job says, "when he has tried me, I will come forth as gold," he means that after his case is heard in heaven, God will vindicate him.[83]

Though Job sought to convince his companions of his righteousness (they were accusing him as advocates of God [Job. 13:6-8]), he really wanted his case heard by the Divine Court. In fact, chapter 31 recounts a legal "oath of innocence" as though Job made his plea before heaven's court. Hear the cry of his heart:

> If only I knew where to find him; if only I could go to his dwelling! I would state my case before him and fill my mouth with arguments. I would find out what he would answer me, and consider what he would say. Would he oppose me with great power? No, he would not press charges against me. There an upright man could present his case before him, and I would be delivered forever from my judge.
> —Job 23:3-7

> Oh, that I had someone to hear me! I sign now my defense—let the Almighty answer me; let my accuser put his indictment in writing… —Job 31:35

Unfortunately, Job's self-righteousness led to his accusation that God acted unjustly toward him[84]— even going so far as to claim that God was his accuser. At this point Job abandoned his advocate's counsel and took his defense into his own hands. God corrected Job in the final chapters, challenging Job from the grounds of divine sovereignty and providence:

> Who has a claim against me that I must pay? Everything under heaven belongs to me. —Job 41:11

In the end, Job was silent; he had learned his lesson: *you cannot bring a lawsuit against God!* God is never unjust.

Nevertheless, we sense throughout the book that Job maintained a legal connection to heaven.[85] For sure, his case was misguided, but his relationship with the court of heaven was authentic. Despite the temptations to focus only on his sorrow, Job directed his attention and affections heavenward. When Job joined in the ministry of heaven—when he prayed for his friends—then God prospered Him again (Job 42:10).

It is for us, then, to discover this legal connection so that we, too, may know the will of God and break the captivity of Satan's kingdom.

Mosaic Covenant Basis for Divine Lawsuits

The Mosaic Covenant stipulations underlie Israel's relationship with God. If Israel disobeyed the covenant terms, the Book of the Law would become a "testimony" in God's court against the rebellious

Israelites. (Similarly, the ark, that contained the law, and the tent, where the ark resided, were called the "ark of the testimony" and "tent of testimony" respectively [Ex. 25:21-22; Nu. 9:15].) The covenant stipulations were the basis of God's lawsuits against the nation:

> After Moses finished writing in a book the words of this law from beginning to end, he gave this command to the Levites who carried the ark of the covenant of the LORD: "Take this Book of the Law and place it beside the ark of the covenant of the LORD your God. There it will remain as a witness against you.
>
> —Deut. 31:24-26[86]

As the nation broke the covenant stipulations, the prophets, as representatives of the Divine Court, brought indictments against Israel for breech of agreement. Scholars often describe these indictments as "lawsuit speech."[87] A lawsuit (Heb. *rîb*) "is an accusation or complaint which an aggrieved party (or advocate acting on behalf of an aggrieved party) makes against one held responsible for the grievance."[88] Both Job and Jeremiah tried unsuccessfully to bring a lawsuit against God.[89] In most cases, however, God is the aggrieved party and the prophets represent Him before the people.

The purpose of the covenant lawsuit was to remind Israel of her obligations and bring her to repentance and restored relationship with God.[90]

Otherwise the consequences of the lawsuit verdict would result. Lawsuit speech was not just a special literary device shared among the prophets, however, but represented the prophet's actual connection to heaven's court.

Joshua's Case Against Israel

When Joshua renewed the Mosaic Covenant at Shechem (Josh. 24; cf. Deut. 31:9-13), he warned the Israelites against future infidelity and of the consequences of severe judgment if they turned from God. At their insistence to remain under God's covenant obligations, Joshua proclaimed them to be witnesses of God:

> Then Joshua said, "You are witnesses against yourselves that you have chosen to serve the LORD." "Yes, we are witnesses," they replied. —Joshua 24:22

Joshua then updated the covenant record and set up a final witness stone as a reminder:

> "This stone will be a witness against us. It has heard all the words the LORD has said to us. It will be a witness against you if you are untrue to your God."
> —Joshua 24:27

Thus Joshua renewed the covenant agreement with Israel and warned them of their legal responsibilities. By doing so, Joshua turned the nation's attention to God their Judge.

Samuel's Case Against Israel

During the later years of Samuel's ministry, the prophet assembled the tribes at Gilgal to confirm Saul as king of the new monarchy (1 Sa. 11:12-12:25). Following the offerings and celebration, the scene took on courtroom overtones and a somber atmosphere when Samuel presented God's lawsuit against them.

Samuel first challenged the Israelites to find any fault with him—to "testify" against him in the presence of witnesses: "Here I stand. Testify against me in the presence of the LORD and his anointed" [King Saul] (1 Sa. 12:3a). When the people answered that no violation could be found, Samuel had the people stand before the "bar of God's justice"[91] and receive God's accusation against them. They were about to learn that they had sinned by demanding a king, for until that time the Lord was their king (1 Sa. 12:12).

Samuel further recited the historical evidence of Israel's guilt for violating the covenant. God then affirmed Samuel's assessment with a miraculous storm (1 Sa. 12:16-18). Convinced of their sin, the people begged Samuel to pray for God's mercy (1 Sa. 12:19). Evidently God rendered an acquittal based on their humility, for Samuel reassured them of God's forgiveness. Nevertheless, the prophet warned them to follow God resolutely (1 Sa. 12:20-25).

This account shows that as God's prophet, and thus heaven's court representative to the people,

Samuel convened an earthly court session in connection with heaven's courtroom. Though the people may have only expected a coronation celebration, heaven directed the assembly into a divine tribunal. Samuel arraigned the people on charges of covenant infidelity and testified against them.

Through all of this, we should note the prophet's close connection to heaven and awareness that his actions were "in the presence of the Lord" (1 Sa. 11:15). In addition, we should note that Samuel fulfilled not only his legal duties as witness and prosecutor, but his advocacy responsibilities as well: "As for me, far be it from me that I should sin against the LORD by failing to pray for you..." (1 Sa. 12:23).

Isaiah's Lawsuit Against Israel

Isaiah brought God's case against Israel in chapter 1:2-3, 1:10-20 and chapters 40-55 of his book. Chapters 40, 44, and 45 appeal to God's sovereignty as the basis of the trial: "Do you not know? Have you not heard? The LORD is the everlasting God, the Creator of the ends of the earth" (Is. 40:28).[92] Since there exists no one greater than God, He affirms His legal decisions with an oath to Himself: "By myself I have sworn, my mouth has uttered in all integrity a word that will not be revoked: Before me every knee will bow; by me every tongue will swear..." (Is. 45:23). His decree is that "all humanity shall come to acknowledge his sovereignty."[93]

Again, in the middle of God's lawsuit, Isaiah used the same language of sovereignty as the courtroom language of Revelation: "I am the first and I am the last" (Is. 48:12; cf. Rev. 1:17; 2:8; 22:13). On the ground of God's foreknowledge and omniscience, God alone makes righteous judgments. He can do this because He simply knows the beginning and the end of all things.

In contrast, idolaters could produce no evidence for their case. Notice how God chided the worshippers of idols:

> Bring in your idols to tell us what is going to happen. Tell us what the former things were, so that we may consider them and know their final outcome. Or declare to us the things to come, tell us what the future holds, so we may know that you are gods. Do something, whether good or bad, so that we will be dismayed and filled with fear. —Is. 41:22-23

"The prophet argued that since Yahweh predicted all that happened, only He is God and the Babylonian gods were patent frauds."[94]

Other chapters present God's lawsuit in courtroom terminology.[95] This lawsuit speech follows a general form:

1. Summons to plead the case:

> Let them [the nations] come forward and speak; let us meet together at the place of judgment. —Is. 41:1

> "Present your case," says the LORD. "Set forth your arguments," says Jacob's King."
> —Is. 41:21

2. Summons given for witnesses and evidence:

> All the nations gather together and the peoples assemble. Which of them foretold this and proclaimed to us the former things? Let them bring in their witnesses to prove they were right, so that others may hear and say, "It is true." "You are my witnesses," declares the LORD, "and my servant whom I have chosen, so that you may know and believe me and understand that I am he. Before me no god was formed, nor will there be one after me."
> —Is. 43:9-10

> Do not tremble, do not be afraid. Did I not proclaim this and foretell it long ago? You are my witnesses. Is there any God besides me? No, there is no other Rock; I know not one. —Is. 44:8

3. Review of the covenant promises and violations (cf. Deut. 27-28). Isaiah 43 contains a litany of promises and judgments summarized in verses 25-28 with a final verdict:

> I, even I, am he who blots out your transgressions, for my own sake, and remembers

your sins no more. Review the past for me, let us argue the matter together; state the case for your innocence. Your first father sinned; your spokesmen [prophets] rebelled against me. So I will disgrace the dignitaries of your temple, and I will consign Jacob to destruction and Israel to scorn. — Is. 43:25-28

4. Declaration of guilt and rendering of a verdict. God judged Judah through the means of exile to Babylon. In the following example, God appeals to the nation to repent. God does this through the metaphor of a call to arise from a drunken stupor. Again, Isaiah uses the symbol of the cup of God's wrath:

Awake, awake! Rise up, O Jerusalem, you who have drunk from the hand of the LORD the cup of his wrath, you who have drained to its dregs the goblet that makes men stagger. —Is. 51:17

Sin is an intoxicating brew, but it poisons everyone who partakes of it with death!

5. Often the context of lawsuit speech contains the promise of divine protection and restoration ("salvation speech"). In effect, God judges in our favor:

But now, this is what the LORD says—he

who created you, O Jacob, he who formed you, O Israel: "Fear not, for I have redeemed you; I have summoned you by name; you are mine..." —Is. 43:1

In the time of my favor I will answer you, and in the day of salvation I will help you; I will keep you and will make you to be a covenant for the people, to restore the land and to reassign its desolate inheritances...
—Is. 49:8

He who vindicates me is near. Who then will bring charges against me? Let us face each other! Who is my accuser? Let him confront me! It is the Sovereign LORD who helps me. Who is he that will condemn me? —Is. 50:8-9a

Jeremiah's Lawsuit Against Judah and Israel

Jeremiah presented a lawsuit against Judah and Israel in chapter 2:4-19. Here he summoned the defendants (Judah and Israel, vs. 4) and indicted them for rebellion and idolatry (vs. 5-8), summarizing their sins with the imagery of a spring and cistern:

My people have committed two sins: They have forsaken me, the spring of living water, and have dug their own cisterns, broken cisterns that cannot hold water.
—Jeremiah 2:13

Here Jeremiah portrays the roots of all rebellion: pride and independence from God. Judah no longer depended on God; the people were no longer what Christ called "poor in spirit" (Mt. 5:3), but had become self-sufficient, following their own way. The result was fatally flawed—their cistern leaked every blessing away.

Thus God brought His people to trial:

> Therefore I bring charges against you again," declares the LORD. "And I will bring charges against your children's children. —Jer. 2:9

Further evidence declared that even other nations had not been so unfaithful to their (false) gods (vs. 10-11). But Israel and Judah had exchanged the glory of God—their Glory—for idols. Heaven groaned as it witnessed the verdict of God, the destruction of Israel and Judah (vs. 12, 15-16).

Amos' Lawsuit Against Israel

The Minor Prophets also contain examples of lawsuit speech revealing Israel's blatant rebellion against God's laws and the subsequent indictments and verdicts from God's court.[96]

Amos 3:1-2 and 9-14 exemplifies the lawsuit process. This passage begins with God's warning against the nation of Israel: "I will call you to account for your iniquities" and ends the lawsuit (inclusio) at 3:14 with the same phrase. The lawsuit shows a court convening and a call to witnesses (vs. 1, 9), the Judge's speech (vs. 2, 10),[97] the indictment (vs. 2, 11), and the sentencing (vs. 11-14).[98]

Amos also cites his credentials as the court messenger who speaks with heaven's authority: God "does nothing without revealing his plan to his servants the prophets" (vs. 7). He then commands the court witnesses to, "Hear this and testify against the house of Jacob" (vs. 13). Amos concludes with a promise of restoration for a remnant:

> As a shepherd saves from the lion's mouth
> only two leg bones or a piece of an ear, so
> will the Israelites be saved. —Amos 3:12a

We should also note Amos' role as intercessor for Israel. Twice he interceded and the Lord spared Israel:

> When they had stripped the land clean, I cried out, "Sovereign LORD, forgive! How can Jacob survive? He is so small!" So the LORD relented. "This will not happen," the LORD said.
> —Amos 7:2-3 (cf. Amos 7:5-6)

From these brief examples we see the prophet's legal basis for bringing charges for breech of covenant. We also see the close connection among the heavenly court, the prophet as advocate and intercessor, and God's people.

Though a remnant remained through God's

judgments, clearly no one could keep all God's requirements nor find permanent acquittal. Condemnation from heaven's court was inevitable.

ENDNOTES

[66] Marjorie Boyle, *The Covenant Lawsuit of the Prophet Amos: III 1 – IV 13*, **Vetus Testamentum** 21 (July 1971), 362.

[67] 1 Kings 22:19; Da. 7:10; Rev. 4:2, 20:11-12.

[68] Ps. 50:1-6; Is. 3:13-26; Is. 43-48; Jer. 2:4-13; Ho. 3:3-17; 4:1-19; Hab. 2.

[69] See, for example, Is. 1:2-3, 10-20; Hos. 3:3-17; 4:1-19; and Micah 6:1-5.

[70] Each messenger may be a divine council representative for each church.

[71] Job 9:33-35; 16:19-21; 19:25; 33:23-24; Da. 7:13-14; Micah 7:9; He. 7:25; 1 Jn. 2:1.

[72] Mal. 3:5; Rev. 1:1-3, 9; 12:17; 19:10; 20:4. As our advocate, Christ also rebuked the accuser: Zech. 3:1-2; Jude 9.

[73] Ex. 18:19; 2 Sa. 24:17; (cf. Acts 2:30); Ezek. 22:30; Amos 7:1-6.

[74] Is. 30:8 ("to serve as a lasting witness"); Da. 7:10; 12:14; Rev. 20:12; cf. Mal. 3:16; Rev. 12-14.

[75] Phillips, 39.

[76] Phillips, 19.

[77] 1 Kings 22:17; Job. 1:12; Ps. 82:1; Is. 3:13; 6:11-13; Ezek. 2:9-3:2; Da. 7:13-14; 26.

[78] See Hab. 2:16; Rev. 14:10; and 16:19.

[79] The Law required double payment for several crimes (Ex. 22:4, 7, 9; Is. 40:2). Symbols of ripe figs (Amos 8:1-3) a measuring basket (Zech. 5:5-11), or a plumb line (2 Kings 21:13; Amos 7:7-9) were also used for God's standard of justice and recompense.

[80] Nu. 20:16; Is. 6:8-9; Ezek. 2:3; Da. 4: 13-14, 17; Hab. 2:2-3; Rev. 1:1-3; 11:3-7; 22:6; cf. Rev. 6:9f; 19:10.

[81] The Antichrist will counterfeit this action in Rev. 13:9 and 14:16.

[82] Ps. 29:1-2; 89:5; 103:20-21; Is. 6:3; Rev. 4:8; 5:9-14.

[83] See David Deuel, *Job 19:25 and 23:10 Revisited: An Exegetical Note*, **Masters Seminary Journal**, vol. 5, no. 1, 1994, 97-99.

[84] Job 9:15-20; 13:18-19; 23:1-7; 40:8.

[85] See also Job 9:32-33; 10:2; 13:6, 17-19; 23:6.

[86] It may be that the Song of Moses (Deut. 32) is an extended lawsuit against Israel.

[87] Sometimes called "complaint speech." According to James Limburg, the verb occurs in the prophets in Is. 3:13; Micah 6:1; Hos. 2:4, 4:4; and Jer. 2:9. The noun occurs in Micah 6:2; Hos. 4:1, 4:4; 12:3; Jer. 25:31. In the majority of Old Testament examples, "the subject of the verb is an aggrieved party making an accusation against an aggrieving party." James Limburg, *The Root Rib and the Prophetic Lawsuit Speeches*, **Journal of Biblical Literature** 88, Sept. 1969, 297. See also the discussion in Leon Morris, *The Biblical Doctrine of Judgement* (Grand Rapids: Eerdmans, 1960) 38-40.

[88] J. Carl Laney, *The Role of the Prophets in God's Case Against Israel*, **Bibliotheca Sacra**, vol. 138, no. 552, October 1981, 318. Lawsuits occurred at the court of the gate, as part of international relations, and as part of God's covenant relations with His people. See James Limburg, *The Root Rib and the Prophetic Lawsuit Speeches*, **Journal of Biblical Literature** 88, Sept. 1969, 291-304.

[89] See Jer. 12:1 and William Holladay, *Jeremiah's Lawsuit With God*, **Interpretation** 17, (July 1963) 280-287.

[90] Is. 44:26; 45:21; 48:20; 49:8f.

[91] Ronald Youngblood, *1 Samuel*, in Frank Gaebelein, general editor, *The Expositor's Bible Commentary*, vol. 3 (Grand Rapids: Zondervan, 1986) 646.

[92] Is. 44:24-28; 45:5-7, 9-10, 12ff.

[93] Geoffrey Grogan, *Isaiah*, in Frank Gaebelein, general editor, *The Expositor's Bible Commentary*, vol. 6 (Grand Rapids: Zondervan, 1986) 272.

[94] Eugene Merrill, *The Literary Character of Isaiah 40-55, Part 2: Literary Genres in Isaiah 40-55*, **Bibliotheca Sacra**, vol. 144, no. 574, April, 1987, 149. See Is. 44:7f. See his useful insights regarding this whole subject.

[95] Is. 41:1-13, 21-29; 43:8-13; 44:6-20; 45:20-21; and 48:12-16.

[96] Ho. 4:4-11:11; 11:12-14:8; Micah 6:1-7:20; Amos 3:1-2, 9-12.

[97] Marjorie Boyle cites Huffmon that the Hebrew word *yada* of Amos 3:2 was used "as a technical term for recognition of the treaty stipulations as binding." See Boyle, 344.

[98] See L. Sinclair, *The Courtroom Motif in the Book of Amos*, **Journal of Biblical Literature** 85, Sept. 1966, 350-353.

3

Courtroom Drama in the New Testament

Christ's redemption answered the indictments of God's lawsuit against humankind (Jn. 15:22-24; Ro. 3:23-24). Those who respond to Christ in faith stand acquitted from the judgment merited by their sins. In fact, Isaiah prophesied that vindication is the heritage of the servants of the Lord: "you will refute every tongue that accuses you" (Is. 54:17).

In the New Testament, a faith-response to the gospel sets up a legally approved relationship to God (or salvation; Col. 2:13-15; He. 9:11-28). In addition, the inward ability of the Holy Spirit now enables us to keep the "righteous requirements of the law" (Ro. 8:4), something the Mosaic Law could not provide.

As we shall see, the writers of the New Testament were well aware of the legal language and courtroom drama surrounding our relationship to God.

John's Gospel as Courtroom Drama

The apostle John made extensive use of legal language in his Gospel (e.g., verdict, testify/witness, Advocate, convict, Judge, guilt, judgment, etc.). John casts his purpose (to prove Jesus' identity as the Christ (Jn. 20:30-31; cf. Jn. 19:35; 21:24) in the framework of courtroom drama. In fact, the trial theme dominates the book.[99] In a sense, John's prologue acts as an opening trial summary statement for Christ, the evidence for its claims to be proven by the witnesses that testify for Him.

Witnesses provide attestation to establish claims as true or false. John marshaled numerous witnesses to prove Christ's identity as the Son of God (Jn. 1:14-15; 20:31). Old Testament Scriptures, the confirmation of the Father, Christ's words and miracles, as well as the witnesses of others (Jn. 5:28-47; 6:27), left the world "without excuse" (Jn. 12:47-48; 15:22-25).[100]

Christ always proved the truth of His testimony. For instance, when Christ claimed to be the Bread of Life, He fed the multitudes (Jn. 6). When He claimed to be the Light of the world, He healed the blind man (Jn. 9). He could call Himself the Good Shepherd because He laid down His life for the sheep (Jn. 10). As the consummate Resurrection and Life, He raised Lazarus from death (Jn.11), which had no hold on Him.

These testimonies not only build God's case for Christ, but also God's case against unbelievers. Several scholars have characterized chapters 1-12 as a "lawsuit of Christ's public ministry" presented against those who reject Christ:

> The lawsuit of the ministry implies that Jesus confronts men with a choice (9:39 ; cf. 3:19). When evidence is offered for the claims of Christ, men must decide for or against Him, and by their choice they judge themselves.[101]

On the surface John's Gospel places Christ on trial, but just beneath that we see humankind before the Judge.[102] Christ has presented His case: "If I had not come and spoken to them, they would not be guilty of sin. Now, however, they have no excuse for their sin" (Jn. 15:22). The evidence is clear. Christ is the Son of God, the Savior of the world. Humankind has been arraigned and sentenced. Somewhere in the eternal heavenlies, God's great gavel of justice has struck for all time. Now the Judge has given Christ the power to carry out the sentencing (Jn. 5:22, 27). The only thing that stands in the way of eternal punishment is the offering of Christ's life for ours. Will humankind accept the commuted sentence?

Courtroom Drama in Acts

Though a predominant theme in John's Gospel (and in John's Revelation, as we shall see), courtroom ministry also permeates Luke's record of the Acts of the Apostles. Luke combines the concrete evidence of eyewitness accounts, the testimony of Old Testament scripture (Acts 2:17-21; 25-29; 7:2ff; 13:16ff; 17:2; 28:23), and many "convincing proofs" (Acts 1:3; 3:16; 4:33; 13:9-12; 14:3; 19:11)—primarily of the Holy Spirit—to substantiate the Christ event.

This represents more than simple evangelism, for Luke couches the apostolic mission in the terminology of the courtroom. For instance, the disciples were "witnesses of everything he did" (Acts 10:39; cf. 10:41; 13:30; 18:5), "all the prophets testify about him" (Acts 10:43), and the Holy Spirit is a joint witness: "We are witnesses of these things, and *so is the Holy Spirit*, whom God has given to those who obey him" (Acts 5:32). As court advocate, the Holy Spirit adds His convicting power to the testimony of the disciples (Acts 2:37) to bring about conversion.

During his court appearance before Festus and King Agrippa, Paul declared:

> But I have had God's help to this very day, and so I stand here and testify to small and great alike. I am saying nothing beyond what the prophets and Moses said would happen—that the Christ would suffer and, as the first to rise from the dead, would proclaim light to his own people and to the Gentiles. —Acts 26:22-23

The word "witnessing" [103] here serves a dual role due to its forensic nature. Paul uses it to describe both his testifying before the Roman procurator and the testimony of the Gospel. The first context is the Roman court of law; the second context reveals his role as a representative of heaven's court.

Being witnesses of the resurrection is the clarion mission of the disciples (Acts 1:8, 22; 2:31-32; 3:15; 13:30, 37; 17:3). Paul was personally charged by the Lord to "be a witness to all men of what you have seen and heard" (Acts 22:15; cf. 23:11; 26:16), a charge that was summarized by Paul himself:

> However, I consider my life worth nothing to me, if only I may finish the race and complete the task the Lord Jesus has given me—the task of testifying to the gospel of God's grace. —Acts 20:24

The disciples' message often contained language of the court. For example, Jesus "is the one whom God appointed as judge of the living and the dead" (Acts 10:42) and Paul "discoursed on righteousness, self-control and the judgment to come" (Acts 24:25). Indeed, the cosmic trial is never far from Paul's thoughts:

> For he has set a day when he will judge the world with justice by the man he has appointed. He has given proof of this to all men by raising him from the dead.
> —Acts 17:31 (cf. 1 Cor. 15:20f)

The members of the early Church, therefore, had a keen awareness of their role as legal representatives of the court of heaven. Can it not be said that the Church exists to facilitate that witness?

Paul's Legal Metaphors

Paul's use of legal metaphors in his epistles is extensive and well documented.[104] Paul derives from Mosaic, Greek, and Roman law the concepts of (just to name a few) slavery and manumission (Ro. 6:16-22; 1 Cor. 7:21-22; Eph. 4:1; the "yoke" of Gal. 5:1 and 1 Tim. 6:1), citizenship (Eph. 2:19; Phil. 3:20), adoption (Ro. 8:15, 23; 9:4; Gal. 4:5; Eph. 1:5), inheritance (Ro. 8:17; Gal. 3:29-4:7; Eph. 3:6; Titus 3:7), redemption (Ro. 3:24; Eph. 1:7-8; Col. 1:13-14; 1 Tim. 2:5-6 [ransom]; Tit. 2:14), judge, condemn, punisher and judgment seat (Ro. 2:2, 16; 13:2, 4; 14:10; 1 Cor. 11:32; 2 Cor. 5:10; 1 Thess. 4:6), and earnest payments and seals (2 Cor. 1:22; 5:5; Eph. 1:14). Closely associated with our redemption is the concept of righteousness, which is laden with forensic baggage, as God our Judge "declares" us righteous (Ro. 2:13) and "credits" righteousness to us (Ro. 4:22-28; cf. 2 Cor. 5:19).[105]

Though these metaphors derive from the rich legal milieu of his day, they have obvious theological significance, and in many cases Paul ties them to the court of heaven. For instance, our citizenship is *of heaven* (Phil. 3:20; cf. 1 Cor. 15:48) from whence we derive our legal authority. Similarly, judgment for the conduct of our earthly probation occurs before the *throne* (bema) of God. With this latter metaphor, Paul portrays a person standing before the "judicial bench" in heaven.

Paul speaks frequently of judgment, condemnation, punishment, and our heavenly Judge (Ro. 2:5; 14:10; 1 Cor. 4:5; 2 Tim. 4:8). Even Paul's exhortations to Timothy occur before the presence of our judge in heaven (2 Tim. 4:1-2).

Although Paul describes our inheritance more in terms of the broader concept of the Kingdom, such inheritance certainly includes heaven. (Peter specifically says our inheritance awaits us in heaven [1 Pt. 1:4].)

Finally, we are heirs *of God* and co-heirs *with Christ* (Ro. 8:17), as well as slaves *to God* (Ro. 6:22). These verses point us to God in heaven who has legally bound us to Himself as co-beneficiaries of His glory. (On a more practical level, I find interesting Paul's admonition to slave masters that they treat their slaves in light of the judgment of our Master in heaven [Eph. 6:9; Col. 4:1].) Similarly, Paul often pictures our present life as "in Christ" (Eph. 2:6; Col. 3:1, 10), meaning that we, at least partially, enjoy our future, heavenly existence now. This is especially true when we consider that Paul described the Holy Spirit as the earnest and seal guaranteeing what is to come.

We must conclude, then, that Paul's legal metaphors create a theological framework rich in the courtroom drama of heaven.

Revelation as Courtroom Drama

For the sake of understanding the extensive use

of courtroom language in Revelation, the following list of legal terms and ideas establishes the book's legal setting: the divine court, seals, (two) witnesses, judgments, judgment throne, thrones for judgment (Rev. 20:4), messengers (including prophets), record books (including the Book of Life), (court) recorder (Rev. 1:11, 19), redemption (Rev. 5:9; 14:3-4), oath swearing, prayer petition (Rev. 6:10), covenant, "seven eyes," "measuring rod" (Rev. 11:1), "accuser" (Rev. 12:10), sealing of individuals from judgment (Rev. 7:1-8), trumpets, "day of wrath" or "hour of judgment" (Rev. 6:17; 14:7; 16:14), faithful witness (Rev. 1:5; 3:14), true and trustworthy words, and testimony.

Revelation 1:9 to 3:22 may constitute a court investigation since Christ's examination resulted in edicts of evaluation, often containing warning and judgment to the seven churches.[106] In fact, the actual court of heaven sits in session in chapters 4-5, 9 (verse 13), and 20.

The Apostle John fulfills the role of court recorder after he is caught up to heaven to view the courtroom activities and judgments of God. The court instructs him variously to write or refrain from writing what he sees.[107] Thus, Revelation constitutes a prophetic court record and John fulfills the role of a commissioned prophet and court recorder much the same as prophets in the Old Testament.[108] The book he writes—Revelation—remains unsealed and "unveiled" for the Church's edification (Rev. 1:1-3; 22:6-10).

Integral to understanding the judgments of

Revelation is the opening court scene of Revelation 4 and 5. This scene sets the stage for much of the remainder of the book and provides the legal context for the future events recorded in Revelation.

I believe Revelation 4 and 5 reveal the Divine Court convening to consider the issue before it, namely, "Who is worthy to break the seals of the scroll of destiny and unleash the judgments?" based presumably on the testimony contained within it.[109] The council deemed Christ alone as worthy because of His redemptive sacrifice (Rev. 5:9-10). As a result, the seals begin to be broken and judgment dispensed.

Most likely the scroll resembles the one given to Ezekiel from the divine council.[110] On Ezekiel's scroll were written future judgments of the world:

> Then I looked, and I saw a hand stretched out to me. In it was a scroll, which he unrolled before me. On both sides of it were written words of lament and mourning and woe. —Ezekiel 2:9-10

The difference in this case is that a hand unrolled Ezekiel's scroll for him. In contrast, seven seals secured the scroll in Revelation 5. People of ancient days stamped seals on legal documents to verify that the contents had not been opened and altered. These seals held a string in place that wound around the scroll to keep it closed. When the person who attached the seal broke it, the string underneath the seal released so that the scroll could be opened.[111]

All heaven waited in anticipation for the breaking

of the seals. Without the testimony contained in the scroll, the judgment/deliverance/worship process could not begin. Thus, the court cannot dispense judgments until after the breaking of each seal.

The actions set in motion by this court session in Revelation 4-5 continue through the seals, trumpets, and bowls. For instance, the breaking of the first four seals unleashes four horsemen who dispatch judgments on earth from the divine council (much the same as the horsemen of Zechariah 1:7-11 patrolled the earth to examine it just prior to judgment). Similarly, the seven angels with the seven plagues come from the temple in heaven, and a voice—probably from the divine council—directs the seven angels to dispense the "seven bowls of God's wrath on the earth" (Rev. 16:1).

The rest of Revelation reveals the legal testimony of Christ (Rev. 5:9-10; Rev. 12-14) and the actions based on the court's decisions.[112] Revelation ends with the final actions of the court (Rev. 20:11f) preceding the new creation and the consummation of God's redemptive plans.

Court Testimony in Revelation

John wrote the book of Revelation as an unveiling of Christ's testimony and the impact of that testimony on the future:

> The revelation of Jesus Christ, which God gave him to show his servants what must soon take place. He made it known by sending his angel to his servant John, who

testifies to everything he saw—*that is, the word of God and the testimony of Jesus Christ*. Blessed is the one who reads the words of this prophecy, and blessed are those who hear it and take to heart what is written in it, because the time is near.

—Revelation 1:1-3

Since Revelation *is prophecy* (Rev. 19:10; 22:7, 10, 18-19) and "the *testimony of Jesus* is the spirit of prophecy" (Rev. 19:10)—that is, prophecy primarily *consists of* Christ's testimony—then it follows that Revelation is primarily an unveiling of Christ's testimony (Rev. 1:2, 9; 12:17; 19:10 [2x]; 20:4).[113]

I believe the Divine Council acts on the testimony of Christ by rendering judgments based on His word.[114] The question remains, "Where does Revelation record Christ's testimony?" Certainly we find it revealed to the seven churches, but this contains only a small portion of the Apocalypse. The elders and living creatures proclaim His testimony in Revelation 5:9-10, but here again this represents a comparatively small amount for a book that is the testimony of Christ.

As I mentioned earlier, we may discover Christ's specific testimony in Revelation 12-14 where we find a litany of events portraying the struggle between the Kingdom of Heaven and Satan's kingdom. These events are dramatized in seven vignettes. (We must realize that what John sees and describes is a drama, not a documentary or history lesson. The symbols represent events in vision/theatrical form, often omitting details or summarizing events. If we try to make a complete, precise correlation, we will err by imposing historic genre on vision/dramatic genre.)[115]

Based on this testimony, which may be the contents of the scroll, judgments will be pronounced and delivered. In other words, the scroll records Christ's testimony upon which the Divine Council in heaven renders its judgments.

The court also reserves witnesses and sends witnesses to the earth. For example, the court sends two witnesses to prophesy (declare the court verdict of impending judgment) to the nations and to bring judgment (dispense court action, Rev. 11:3-12).

The court seals 144,000 witnesses (Rev. 7:1-8; 14:1-5), and validates their testimony by the stamp of the name of the Father and Son (Rev. 14:1) and perhaps preserving them from judgments to come. They also become, in a sense, sequestered for the court, for "they follow the Lamb wherever he goes" (Rev. 14:4). Their testimony was validated as pure and truthful, since they "did not defile themselves with women, for they kept themselves pure" (Rev. 14:4) and since no "lie was found in their mouths; they are blameless" (Rev. 14:5). Consequently, the 144,000 may not be evangelists in any sense of the term. Their purpose has to do with the court of heaven, and perhaps only indirectly with earth in terms of the consequences of their testimony.

Many expositors equate these witnesses with evangelists, but this interpretation ignores the possibility that the witnesses play a different role for the court, perhaps as humankind's confirmation of Christ's testimony or of the evils they suffered. No further human witnesses will be needed since the 144,000 constitute the perfect, complete number.[116]

Unfortunately, most popular perspectives of Revelation focus primarily on earthly events, rather than on the activities of heaven. Christians concern themselves far too much with making Revelation fit current events. Revelation is far more concerned with heaven—its courtroom testimony and decrees—than with the identity of the antichrist or the construction of a new temple in Jerusalem.

Just as the Old Testament court scenes depicted future events, so Revelation does as well. When we understand that much of what happens in Revelation is either a part of the heavenly court itself or a direct result of the council decisions, then the events in that book come into perspective.

The Final Court Day

Prophets have long anticipated a final day of recompense. Termed "the Day" or "the Day of the Lord" (e.g., Amos 2:16; 3:14; 5:18-20),[117] this phrase became paradigmatic of humankind's last court day. The Day of the Lord denotes at least three things:

1. The near events of judgment and restoration of the nation of Israel.

2. The "last days" of the Church age (cf., Amos 9:11; Acts 2:17; 15:16-18) where the future kingdom already breaks into the now (in

overlapping ages).

3. The actual, final "supreme court" session of Revelation 19-20 following the parousia of Christ and prior to the commencement of the eternal states.

When Paul explained the significance of this third aspect to the Thessalonians, he used a "matrix of forensic terms" that portrayed an "eschatological day in court"[118] in which the persecuted would be vindicated:

All this is *evidence* [legal exhibit] *that God's judgment is right*, and as a result you will be counted worthy of the kingdom of God, for which you are suffering. God is just: He will pay back trouble to those who trouble you and give relief to you who are troubled, and to us as well. This will happen when the Lord Jesus is revealed from heaven in blazing fire with his powerful angels. —2 Thess. 1:5-7

Concerning the coming of our Lord Jesus Christ and *our being gathered to him* [a legal assembly], we ask you, brothers, not to become easily unsettled or alarmed by some prophecy, report or letter supposed to have come from us, saying that *the day of the Lord* [court day] has already come.
—2 Thess. 2:2

Paul further described "that Day" as a day of "God's wrath, when his righteous judgment will be revealed. God 'will give to each person according to what he has done'" (cf., Ps. 62:12; Prov. 24:12). All of our works will be tested and revealed by fire (1 Cor. 3:13).

The Great White Throne judgment follows Christ's second coming. God will make final decisions based on the books (of testimony) and the Book of Life (Rev. 20:11-15). Everyone must "give an account" on this day (Mt. 12:36), and "by your words you will be acquitted, and by your words you will be condemned" (Mt. 12:37).

ENDNOTES

[99] Jn. 1:32; 3:18-19, 31-32, 35-36; 5:28-40; 7:7; 8:12-18, 50, 54; 12:47-48; 15:22-25; 16:7-11. John uses the noun for "witness" fourteen times and the verb thirty-three times in his Gospel—more than any other New Testament writer does. See also 1 Jn. 2:1 and 5:6.

[100] Dale Glass-Hess, the editor of my paper, reminded me that Peter used several lines of evidence, or "witnesses," to prove that Christ was the Messiah in his speech on the Day of Pentecost: "1) the evidence of Scripture (Acts 2:16-21); 2) the evidence of personal experience (Acts 2:32); the evidence of history and current events (Acts 2:22, 29); and 4) the evidence of conscience (Acts 2:37)."

[101] Allison Trites, *The Woman Taken in Adultery*, **Bibliotheca Sacra**, vol. 131, no. 522, April 1974, 141.

[102] Sometimes called "the lawsuit of the Last Day." See A. A. Trites, *Witness*, in Green, Joel G.; McKnight, Scot; Marshall, I.

Howard; editors, *Dictionary of Jesus and the Gospels*, (Downer's Grove, IL: InterVarsity Press, 1998) 880.

103 The Greek participle μαρτυρόμενος.

104 See, for instance, Francis Lyall, *Slaves, Citizens, Sons: Legal Metaphors in the Epistles* (Grand Rapids: Zondervan, 1984) and the respective entries and bibliographies in G. Hawthorne, R. Martin, D. Reid, general editors, *Dictionary of Paul and His Letters* (Downers Grove: InterVarsity Press, 1993) and L. Ryken, J. Wilhoit, and T. Longman III, general editors, *Dictionary of Biblical Imagery* (Downers Grove: InterVarsity Press, 1998).

105 See the discussion regarding righteousness in Thomas Schreiner, *Paul: Apostle of God's Glory in Christ* (Downers Grove: InterVarsity Press, 2001) 189-217.

106 The "seven stars" in the right hand of Christ (Rev. 1:16, 20) are the "messengers" of the seven churches in Asia Minor. These messengers are probably the representatives of those churches before the divine council. They are sent with the specific covenant judgment/warning scrolls to each of the churches.

107 Rev. 1:11, 19; 10:4; 14:13; 19:9; 21:5.

108 See Isaiah 6:8 and Ezekiel 2-3.

109 I am indebted to R. Dean Davis for this idea as well as the insight of prophets as court witnesses (cf. p. 105). See R. Dean Davis, *The Heavenly Court Judgment of Revelation 4-5* (New York: University Press of America, 1992) 167-168. As a Seventh-day Adventist, however, Davis takes his conclusions too far in his final chapter (pp. 217-231). This is unfortunate, as his book is otherwise very insightful and useful. For a discussion regarding the aberrant Seventh-day Adventist view of "investigative judgment," see Walter Martin, *The Kingdom of the Cults* (Minneapolis: Bethany House Publishers, 1985) 476-480.

110 The book given to the Lamb was a scroll called an

"opisthograph" because it had writing "on both sides" (Rev. 5:1). There are different views of the nature of the scroll the text refers to. For example, some believe it could be like the title deed that Jeremiah used to purchase a field (Jer. 32:9-25). Such deeds have been found with seven seals. See Massyngberde Ford, *Revelation*, Anchor Bible (Garden City, NY: Doubleday, 1975) 92.

[111] A sealed, legal scroll was to be opened only by the one who sealed it, thus guaranteeing its validity. It is quite possible that the scroll given to the Lamb was *His* scroll with *His* seals (the number seven representing perfect witness rather than seven different witnesses). In other words, the seals could only be opened by Christ because He put them there.

[112] Revelation 7:2; 9:13-14; 10:4, 8; 11:12; 12:10; 14:13, 15, 18; 16:1, 17; 18:4; 19:5, 17; 21:3.

[113] There are nineteen occurrences of the word "testimony" (or witness; Greek "marturion" or "martus") and its cognates in Revelation. The phrase "spirit of prophecy" may be a Jewish expression for "prophecy." See note 3.1 Church Order under the entry for Prophecy, Prophets, and False Prophets in Ralph P. Martin and Peter H. Davids, editors, *Dictionary of the Later New Testament and Its Development* (Downers Grove: InterVarsity Press, 1997).

[114] Rev. 7:2; 9:13-14; 14:15, 18; 16:1; 19:17.

[115] For instance, the woman, though one figure, probably represents many. The manchild (representing Christ) is immediately caught up to the throne after birth, bypassing the events of Christ's death, burial, and resurrection. For the purposes of the drama, these events were simply not mentioned. We should not make too much of this, as apocalyptic genre does not require complete details and this important part of Christ's testimony is mentioned elsewhere (Rev. 5:9-10).

[116] The number 144,000 derives from the 12,000 selected from each tribe. Elsewhere in Revelation the number 12 has symbolic meaning, probably representing completion (Rev. 21:16-

17; 22:2).

[117] See also Is. 2:12-21; 13:9-11; Jer. 46; Ezek. 7:19; Joel 3:14-16; Obad. 16-21; Mal. 4:5.

[118] For example, ἡμέρᾳ (2 Thess. 1:10; 2:2) is a court day, ἔνδειγμα (2 Thess. 1:5) is a court exhibit, ἐπισυναγωγῆς ἐπ αὐτὸν (2 Thess. 2:1) signifies a legal assembly. These ideas were taken from a paper by Terry Wilder that was delivered at the November, 1999, Evangelical Theological Society meeting in Danvers, MA. In similar fashion, Paul declared that we must all appear before the judgment seat of Christ (2 Cor. 5:10).

4

Sharing in the Courtroom Ministry of Heaven

The courtroom ministry of heaven includes all God's legal actions and messages. We don't know how often the court of heaven convenes to consider legal matters, but we do know Christ's advocacy ministry continues unabated. In addition, we know (from God's lawsuit brought against the nation of Israel by Hosea) that God revealed how sins concern Him continually:

> …but they do not realize that I remember all their evil deeds. Their sins engulf them; they are always before me. —Ho. 7:2

Further, we know that Christ evaluates each local church (Rev. 2-3) and desires to correct and guide the members of each, sending edicts and directives via messengers, prophets, and prophecy. Thus, God's courtroom ministry fills a prominent place in His activities.

Though God is sovereign and thoroughly just in all His decisions, He still desires to share this on-going courtroom ministry of heaven. How amazing that God, though omniscient and immutable, allows others to participate in His activities! Perhaps in some small way, the manner in which a father desires a son to be with him or to follow in his steps reflects this same longing God has toward us. In turn, as His sons, God puts something in our spiritual DNA that longs to be with our heavenly Father. The result is that the whole process of sharing in God's ministry reproduces God's image in us. When we are with Him, we learn to be like Him.

Some of what we learn is how to emulate God's holiness, justice, and mercy (cf. Ro. 8:29). We learn how Christ pleads for others with earnestness, empathy, and steadfastness. We learn how to make reasonable, moral judgments. We gain the confidence of knowing His will—a confidence that doesn't accept defeat. In short, we share in His courtroom ministry. How sad that much of the Church denies that a God of love brings judgment! How far removed from the ministry of Christ it has come!

Entrance Into the Heavenlies

Having ascended to heaven, Christ opened a way

for us to enter heaven and participate in its on-going activity:

> For Christ did not enter a man-made sanctuary that was only a copy of the true one; he entered heaven itself, now to appear for us in God's presence. —He. 9:24[119]

> Therefore, brothers, since we have confidence to enter the Most Holy Place by the blood of Jesus, by a new and living way opened for us through the curtain, that is, his body, and since we have a great priest over the house of God, let us draw near to God with a sincere heart in full assurance of faith, having our hearts sprinkled to cleanse us from a guilty conscience and having our bodies washed with pure water.
> —He. 10:19-22

We have access to the heavenly life by following our trailblazer into the heavenlies through prayer. The leading of the Holy Spirit enables our prayers to ascend into the heavenlies.

Paul described this connection with the concept of being "in Christ"—raised with Him and seated with Him in heavenly places (Eph. 1:20; 2:6). Though this is a spiritual concept, it is a reality. Since we are in Christ, our position allows us to share in His present ministry. Prayer transports us into heaven where we share in Christ's intercessory/advocacy ministry and present our requests according to the will of God the Judge.

Thus, all believers have access to heaven's court-room through their connection to Christ, who is the Head of the Body and our personal advocate in heaven. Here we can understand His heart, His prayers, and His will for us. Here we access our solutions to all kinds of problems and find authority to overcome the kingdom of darkness:

> This is the confidence we have in approach-ing God: that if we ask anything according to his will, he hears us. And if we know that he hears us—whatever we ask—we know that we have what we asked of him.
> —1 Jn. 5:14-15

> His intent was that now, through the church, the manifold wisdom of God should be made known to the rulers and authorities in the heavenly realms, accord-ing to his eternal purpose which he accom-plished in Christ Jesus our Lord.
> —Eph. 3:10-11

Our prayers, in concert with Christ's, struggle "against the rulers, against the authorities, against the powers of this dark world and against the spiri-tual forces of evil in the heavenly realms" (Eph. 6:12).[120] We prevail through union with Christ's ministry!

Prayer Petitions

Presenting our needs and interceding on behalf of others—presenting our case before the Judge—leads us to a special kind of legal prayer: *a petition.*

> Do not be anxious about anything, but in everything, by prayer and petition, with thanksgiving, present your requests to God. —Phil. 4:6[121]

I hope to show that a petition[122] contains the following basic elements:

1. An issue or need.
2. An appeal, often based on a promise or precedent.
3. If possible, multiple witnesses who offer the petition in agreement.

The Bible records several such petitions:[123]

> Therefore confess your sins to each other and pray for each other so that you may be healed. —Ja. 5:16a

> When he opened the fifth seal, I saw under the altar the souls of those who had been slain because of the word of God and the testimony they had maintained. They called out in a loud voice, "How long, Sovereign Lord, holy and true, until you judge the inhabitants of the earth and

avenge our blood?" —Rev. 6:9-10

In Matthew 18:19-20, Christ tied the need for multiple witnesses to our prayer petitions:

> "Again, I tell you that if two of you on earth agree about anything you ask for, it will be done for you by my Father in heaven. For where two or three come together in my name, there am I with them." —Mt. 18:19-20

The "two in agreement" concept establishes the legal setting of this context. A testimony requires at least two to substantiate it (Deut. 19:15; 1 Cor. 13:1; 1 Tim. 5:19). However, the NIV translation "agree about anything you ask for" loses the legal terminology of the text. The Greek word "pragmatos" (matter, practice) has to do with *legal matters* in such contexts. D. A. Carson noted:

> Scripture is rich in prayer promises…but if this passage deals with prayer at all, it is restricted by the context and by the phrase *peri pantos pragmatos* (NIV, "about anything"), which should here be rendered "about any judicial matter…"[124]

Christ speaks not so much about prayer in the general sense here, but specifically regarding petitioning the Father about judicial matters (e.g., the "binding" or "loosing" of judgment against a brother who sins [Mt. 18:18]). While we may categorize petitions under the general heading of prayer, I believe petitions apply more specifically to requests made from our legal authority as God's representatives or "witnesses." Since courtroom testimony required multiple witnesses, it makes sense that believers should offer petitions in agreement among one another.

In addition, the necessity of agreement in Christ's name conjoins our purposes with His. By allowing others to judge what we say, we help ensure exactness and authenticity (as also with prophecy). On the other hand, without this agreement, our petitions have no legal standing in heaven's court. Thus, the verse also implies that the testimony of two *in agreement with Christ's ministry in heaven* guarantees that the Judge will answer a petition.

Offering petitions to our advocate also fulfills a critical concept in spiritual warfare. When the court decides in our favor, the tide of battle turns to our victory (Da. 7:21-26). Such favor comes in response to our petitions. Paul notes this in his lengthy explanation of the armor of God and spiritual warfare in Ephesians 6:10-20. He concludes his discussion with an admonition to pray, twice using the term for a petition:[125]

> With all prayer and petition pray at all times in the Spirit, and with this in view, be on the alert with all perseverance and petition for all the saints.
> —Eph. 6:18 (NAS)

This truth was brought home to me very clearly by an example of spiritual warfare related to me by my mother. Before moving to Atlanta, my mother and father needed to sell their house in Anchorage, Alaska. At that time the economy was in a slump, and homes were not selling well. My mother gave the prayer need to a prophet at their church, and both committed it to prayer. Late one night, my mother was awakened by a thump on the roof of the house. An angel appeared to her as she lay in bed. The angel was wearing work overalls and wrung his hands together, as though wiping dirt from them. He said, "I have killed all the foes that have come against selling the house." At that moment my mother had a vision of many dead demons lying all over the yard. For a year my mother had peace about the sale of their home. It eventually sold at the end of that year—right on time.

Three other important factors figure in the process of offering petitions to the Father. First of all, we should note that Christ presented His petitions not according to His will, but according to the Father's will (e.g., Jn. 17:7, 11-12, 15). In the same way, the Holy Spirit "intercedes for the saints *according to the will of God"* (Ro. 8:27). If Christ and the Holy Spirit present requests in this manner, how much more must we first ascertain God's will before making our requests!

We now have confidence in approaching God with our petitions:

> …that if we ask anything according to his

will, he hears us. And if we know that he hears us—whatever we ask—we know that we have what we asked of him.

—1 Jn. 5:14-15

Secondly, as advocates sharing in Christ's ministry, we must be careful not to accuse others to the Father. Nothing could be farther from the heart of Christ for His Church—His Bride—than to play the role of accuser of the brethren (Ro. 14:1-4). Satan performed that role until Christ removed him from heaven. How could we want to continue it? Our calling is one of empathy and support, following the role of our advocate.

Thirdly, when we ask anything of God, we must come to Him out of a sense of real need. Christ meant this when He taught in the Beatitudes, "Blessed are the poor in spirit, for theirs is the kingdom of heaven" (Mt. 5:3). To be "poor in spirit" means that we recognize our dependence on the Lord. In fact, the Greek word for "petition" derives from the verb meaning "to want or to lack" and may imply that such petitions spring from a feeling of want.[126]

God's provision is both inexhaustible and available to those who ask in faith according to His will. George Whitefield once said, "The bank of heaven is a sure bank. I have drawn thousands of bills upon it, and never had one sent back protested."[127]

Gifts of the Spirit

The Holy Spirit brings gifts or "gracings" called

the charismata (Ro. 12:6-8; 1 Cor. 12:4-11; Eph. 4:11-13; 1 Pt. 4:10-11). God designed these gifts partly to reveal what is on the heart of Christ—to connect us with Christ's current ministry in heaven. As Christ said, the Holy Spirit will "take from what is mine and make it known to you" (Jn. 16:14),[128] including things to come (Jn. 16:13, an obvious reference to prophecy). In other words, the charismata are one of the means by which Christ has expression in this world and where the courtroom ministry takes effect in and among believers.

In a very real sense, then, the operation of the charismata is an extension of the current intercessory/advocacy ministry of Christ in heaven. During our communion with Christ, the Holy Spirit communicates to us the desires on Christ's heart and gives us the enablement to effect His will.

It is therefore imperative that we be able to hear from Christ. Before the gifts can operate, we must be able, like Jeremiah, to ascend into the council of the Lord (Jer. 23:18, 22). The key to using the gifts is the ability to recognize His voice through the enablement of the Holy Spirit. The more we know Christ intimately, the more frequent and accurate will be the operation of the gifts in our lives.

Being used in prophecy, for instance, is not so much a matter of "getting a word" as positioning oneself (through prayer, worship, and reading the Bible) to hear His words. Since the "testimony of Jesus is the spirit of prophecy" (Rev. 19:10), then prophecy should reflect Christ's past testimony (Jn. 3; Rev. 12) and His current testimony before the

Divine Court.[129] It should include such things as Christ's desires, will, concerns, purpose, compassion, mercy, authority, and power all in specific application. It should compel us, transform us, encourage us, teach us, and comfort us according to His will.

Our connection with heaven is far more dynamic, far more vibrant, than we can imagine. Prayer time is not just an endurance test, but an opportunity to participate in something powerful, transforming, and revolutionary. Paul declared:

> We have not received the spirit of the world but the Spirit who is from God, that we may understand what God has freely given us. —1 Corinthians 2:12

The result is that the life of Heaven now dwells within the corporate Body through the presence of the Holy Spirit.

The Power of a Godly Imagination

Our connection to heaven involves more than our Spirit-inspired prayer bond or manifestations of His gifts. It also entails the use of a sanctified imagination. Without this precious, innate ability to picture heaven in our minds, most of our prayers would be dull and lifeless. The imagination is the catalyst of the spirit, helping us visualize the heavenly realms. Our imagination enables us to picture heaven's courtroom where we present our cases to God on his throne.

Particularly helpful here are the passages in the Bible that depict heaven. Scripture describes fantastic, beautiful scenes that capture consecrated imaginations with a sense of awe and wonder. Earthly courtrooms cannot begin to measure the glory of their heavenly counterpart. The images of an emerald rainbow (Rev. 4:3), the incredible living creatures (Rev. 4:6-8), the lightning (Rev. 4:5), and the throne of God on a platform of glass (Rev. 4:6a) should inspire our thoughts and foster more fervent prayers.

During our worship services, we have used multi-media and special lighting effects to enhance worship and relate to the younger generation. Though our special effects are considerably tame compared to contemporary youth concerts, the lighting presents a real adjustment to many. Nevertheless, my response has been to say, "If you want a real light show, just visit heaven!" Can you imagine the emanating glory of God, the bursts of lightning, and all of this reflecting off a sea of glass? If God enjoys it, why shouldn't we?

Even so, the imagination should not be limited to such majestic, forceful images. Often simple scenes of walking hand-in-hand with Christ, lying at His feet, or leaning on His breast as John did, can be just as valuable. There are times, especially of sorrow and failure, when the imagination needs to rest in images that convey a sense of Christ's peace and individual attention. Christ *personally* petitioned the Father for Peter and *personally* comforted him as Peter's advocate (Lk. 22:31-32). He cares for each of us just as much.

The imagination is a wondrous gift given by Him who is the greatest Imaginer of all. When it becomes part of Spirit-led prayers, it is a powerful benefit for our pleadings.

Unfortunately, the gifts of the Spirit often lie dormant because our imaginations are filled with ungodly pictures from hours of watching TV and videos. Intimacy with God maintains a pure imagination and clears the way for a prophetic connection with heaven.

The Prophetic Connection With the Court

Since the activity of heaven's court continues at least until the Great White Throne, prophecy should be rich in the terminology of the Divine Court. Sadly, most prophecy lacks this today. I find that whenever I speak a prophetic word with forensic terms and symbols, God adds a special "anointing" to the word. Such phrases as "God decides in our favor," "argues our case," "sends an edict," or that He "stands by us to convict the world," stirs hearts because we have tapped into the language of heaven.

Lest we regard lawsuit speech as insipid legal terminology, we should remember that the prophets spoke *poetically*, touching the deep pathos of God's heart. In effect, they expressed their messages as *poetic lawsuits*. The language of God's legal actions with humankind often consists of vivid, penetrating, and fervent speech—almost desperate at times:

> For a long time I have kept silent, I have been quiet and held myself back. But now,

> like a woman in childbirth, I cry out, I gasp
> and pant.—Is. 42:14

In addition to the terms we use, prophetic revelation includes what the Holy Spirit causes us to "see and hear." The prophetic consciousness must be filled with an awareness of heaven and Christ's current ministry. Without this, prophecy lacks the ability to "cut through the numbness, to penetrate the self-deception"[130] of society.

In other words, prophecy (and all the charismata) springs from our connection to heaven. It has nothing to do with psychic phenomena. When prophecy taps directly into what God decides and directs, the power of the Kingdom of Heaven breaks into this world.

This is especially true when we know God's heart for specific individuals, whether believers or unbelievers. As Christ intercedes for us on a regular basis, He invites us to share in His ministry. Sharing in this means that we present our petitions according to His will and join His intercessions for the Church. As He stirs our hearts with His burdens, He reveals words of knowledge, words of wisdom, and prophecy.

We can place ourselves in a better position to hear God's prophetic words by asking the right questions. (I call this prophetic posturing.) We should begin by asking Christ, "What is on your heart?" Or perhaps more specifically, "What is on your heart for this person? How are you praying for him or her?" This enables us to become quiet and listen, thus connecting our hearts to His current ministry of intercession.

Not long ago I felt deep concern for a member of our church who was facing heart surgery. Early the next morning, I received a spiritual dream to pray for her and anoint her with oil according to James 5:14. The dream very specifically directed in the manner in which I was to do this. Our senior pastor and I prayed for her, anointing her with oil. During the examination, the doctors determined that she had 30% blockage (or more) in two arteries and 90% blockage in another. She had immediate surgery to correct the worst artery. Several months later she began to have other problems in her left shoulder and arm and went to the hospital for a check up. I prayed for her again and anointed her with oil. She felt at that moment that God had finished His healing work and that she would not need additional surgery. The tests revealed that she was improving in the two arteries that were not corrected. She had "no significant stenosis" (or blockage) in one artery and "mild, 20% to 30% stenosis" in the other. We believe that she will continue to improve.

There are other times in ministry where our connection to heaven plays a vital role. Whenever I prepare a eulogy for a funeral, for instance, I close my office door and quietly pray. I don't begin writing until I hear the burden of Christ's heart. Often I weep as I write because of the emotion. Even during those times when I've written a eulogy for someone I didn't know, God has directed me by revealing His heart. Often the accuracy of the words I write was later confirmed by those who knew the deceased. I may not have known the person, but God did and knows just what needs to be said to comfort the family.

Not only should we link our hearts with Christ for individuals, but we also should offer a second level of questions, "What is on your heart for this church? What do you want to say to this church?" With these questions, we specifically request to be the recipient of Christ's message of examination of our church. This corresponds to the courtroom ministry of Christ in Revelation 2-3, where Christ revealed the results of His investigation of the seven churches of Asia Minor to the apostle John. Here we must be cautious, however, for too often the tendency will be to want to judge and criticize out of the emotions of our own hearts, rather than actually discern Christ's evaluations and intercessions. Unfortunately, prophecy sometimes becomes a "soap box" for anyone to articulate a personal grievance to the church.

If we approach sermon preparation by first seeking Christ's heart for our church, our messages will take on new life. In a very real sense, each message should be a letter from Christ postmarked from heaven to the local church. People don't come to church to see me, or to hear an excellent sermon. They come for an encounter with God. They want to hear what He is saying.

A third set of questions can be asked to provide insight as to Christ's heart for the nations: "What is your desire for this country? What are its people's needs? What are you saying to its leaders?" (To this end, an excellent resource is the "Operation World" prayer guide by Patrick Johnstone and Jason Mandryk and published by Operation Mobilization. Up to date and filled with meticulous detail, this resource is rich in practical information to help our prayers for the nations.)

We can all share in His general will for the salvation of souls in every nation, but strategic intercession can change the course of history! Such was the case in Israel where three key intercessors, Solomon (pre-captivity, 2 Kings 8:28ff; 2 Chron. 6:36-39), Daniel (mid-captivity, Da. 9:1-19), and Nehemiah (post-captivity, Neh. 1:1-11), wept, groaned, and petitioned[131] God for the nation. By claiming the promises of the Mosaic Covenant (Deut. 30:1-6), they brought deliverance to the people.

Herein lies an important aspect of making a petition. Covenant promises form the basis for making a legal appeal before the court of heaven. Under the New Covenant, the promises lie within the scope of the kingdom that Christ conferred on His disciples (Lk. 22:29-30). Can it not be said that the terms of the New Covenant consist of nothing less than the inheritance of the Kingdom of Heaven? By giving the Church the "keys of the kingdom" (Mt. 16:19), Christ was giving access to authority and power that belong to heaven itself!

Recently, Dr. Eva Evans, a woman used mightily with the prophetic gift, recounted the following story regarding the tragic events of September 11, 2001:

In June of 1999 I was at the Pentagon with Ruth Heflin and about eight other people. We were walking and praying through certain corridors. Suddenly, Ruth had a vision of a section of the Pentagon. In her vision she saw that wing "crumbling." We decided we should pray for protection for that section and asked several Washington prayer groups to join with us in intercession.

On September 11, we learned that the hijacked plane that hit the Pentagon had actually veered from its flight path causing it to hit the section that, due to construction, had fewer people inside. If it had not veered, it would have exactly hit the area that Ruth saw crumble. Without the prayers of many Christians, the death toll would have been several thousand instead of several hundred.

Only God knows how such intercession has and will affect the outcome of history! Whether petitioning God or prophesying for individuals, churches or nations, our prayers should always maintain a close connection to heaven.

Losing Our Heavenly Connection

We can lose our heavenly connection, however, when we allow sin in our lives. Paul gave an example of this in Colossians where he explained that a prideful teacher cuts himself off from the life flow of Christ:

> *He has lost connection with the Head,*
> from whom the whole body, supported and
> held together by its ligaments and sinews,
> grows as God causes it to grow.
> —Col. 2:19 [emphasis mine]

This literally means that such a person no longer "holds to the Head." Paul may very well be talking about a paralyzed body—a disabled and powerless Church. Sin paralyzes us by removing us from our vital connection with Christ. Through genuine repentance, however, we can regain our ability to determine His will.

No sin breaks our connection to heaven faster than the sin of prayerlessness. As we have seen, Samuel recognized his intercessory responsibility and prayed relentlessly for the nation of Israel. He admitted that failure to do so constituted a grievous sin.

This can be seen in an example from the disciples of Christ. During one mission Christ's disciples rejoiced to have demons subject to them, but then later could not cast one out. Christ responded that the lacking ingredient was prayer (Lk. 10:17; Mk. 9:29; though many manuscripts add "fasting" to Mk. 9:29). Prayer keeps us in tune with the ministry of heaven and enables us to keep in step with the Spirit (Gal. 5:25).

In Conclusion

We have seen that in many cases the Bible uses

legal language to describe God's actions. This makes perfect sense when we recognize the frequent courtroom setting of heaven, its members, and the activities of the Divine Court. Much of Christ's current ministry in heaven as our advocate relates to courtroom jurisprudence. Similarly, much of the Holy Spirit's ministry on earth processes heaven's adjudication as primary advocate against the world.

It is therefore vital that we remain connected to this current judicial ministry. Sharing in Christ's current ministry means that we participate in Christ's advocacy *for* humankind through our petitions and intercessions, and that we bear testimony of God's judgment *against* humankind as witnesses of the cosmic trial of the ages. Without our advocacy or testimony, many souls could be damaged or even lost.

God fosters this connection through the abiding presence of the Holy Spirit, who is our resident advocate and who provides us with the necessary gifts (abilities) to convict the world and strengthen the testimony of the Church.

In this regard, I would like to re-emphasize what I first mentioned in the Introduction, namely, that the courtroom ministry of heaven provides an overarching framework for Pentecostal/Charismatic theology. First of all, this study shows that the charismatic gifts are not isolated phenomena or random blessings, but remain integral to Christ's current advocate/judicial ministry. They provide valuable links to the will of God declared in heaven.

Secondly, we should note that this study shows

the need for the *continuance* of the charismata. The purpose and function of the gifts are rooted in the courtroom ministry of heaven. Thus, they should not be limited to early church history as though (purported by some) they occurred only as an initial validation of the Church by God. While it may be true that God confirmed His initial witness to certain people groups with various signs and wonders, His same witness and judicial ministry continues today.

Thirdly, then, this study demonstrates that, contrary to the aberrant ideas of some Charismatics on the periphery of this movement, the "gifts" are not unrestricted or unconditional means for moving heaven for the benefit of our health and wealth. They are, rather, part of the means to cooperate with the will of heaven and see that will accomplished on earth.

What an incredible thing to have: *access to the activity and ministry of the courtroom of Heaven!* Whether through courtroom edicts, court messengers, angels, prophets, or the ministry of Christ, we can participate in the coming of Christ's kingdom into this world. May our prayers soar into the courtroom of heaven and find assurance in the heart of our blessed advocate!

ENDNOTES

[119] See also He. 1:3.

[120] There remains open hostility between the Church and spiritual forces of evil, though Christ continues exalted and conqueror

over all.

121 Paul clearly delineates prayer and petition here by the use of the definite article: τῇ προσευχῇ καὶ τῇ δεήσει.

122 The Greek word δέησις.

123 Other petitions may include Mt. 9:38; Mt. 24:20; Lk. 22:31-34; Ja. 5:16; Jn. 17:13, 21-23; Mt. 5:20; Eph. 6:18; He. 7:25; Phil. 1:9-11. The Lord's Prayer contains six petitions. It is interesting to note that δέησις occurs frequently in legal contexts in the LXX: Job 8:6; 16:21 (Job's advocate); 27:9; 36:19; Ps. 17[16]:1; 21[20]:2; 33[34]:15; 129[130]:2; 142[143]:1; Lam. 3:55 (note vs. 58).

124 D. A. Carson, *Matthew*, in Frank E. Gaebelein, editor, *The Expositor's Bible Commentary*, vol. 8 (Grand Rapids: Zondervan, 1984) 403.

125 The Greek word δεήσει.

126 See D. Edmond Hiebert, *The Significance of Christian Intercession*, **Bibliotheca Sacra**, vol. 149, no. 593, January, 1992, 17. While editing this paper, Dr. Blackburn pointed out that the very act of "requesting" most often implies a sense of lack.

127 Randy Colver and Cathy Colver, *The Quotable Whitefield: A Sampler of Sayings*, in *George Whitefield: Christian History, Issue 38*, (Carol Stream, IL: Christianity Today, Inc.) 1997.

128 This ministry reflects Christ's earthly ministry of which He said, "The words I say to you are not just my own. Rather, it is the Father, living in me, who is doing his work" (Jn. 14:10).

129 The current testimony should not contradict or be held in the same authority as the testimony of Scripture.

130 Walter Brueggemann, *The Prophetic Imagination* (Philadelphia: Fortress Press, 1978) 49.

131 In both the prayers of King Solomon and Daniel, the LXX uses the word δέησις (petition): 1 Kings [3 Kings] 8:28, 30, 38, 45, 49, 52 (2x), 54; Da 9:3, 17, 23.

A Meditation on Heaven

What will be said for me,
When before the Judge I stand?
What will become of me,
At verdict's harsh demand?
Will my Kinsman and Redeemer—
My Friend be at my side?
Will my advocate consider,
His atonement to provide?
When woes of condemnation,
Echo through the temple gate,
Will my Savior ransom me,
From Hell's eternal fate?
Let now the books be opened,
Find a messenger to run,
For judgment lies commuted,
And His words to me: "Well done!"

LaVergne, TN USA
15 February 2011
216514LV00001B/20/A

9 781591 603801